# Tilted

99: The Press, P.O. Box 956, Lowell, MA 01853.

FIRST EDITION

Designed by Colleen Cole.
Cover image: Louise's Eyeglasses © by Nick Krug, Lawrence, KS.

Library of Congress Cataloging-in-Publication Data has been applied for.

ISBN: 978-0-9882662-8-5

# Tilted

## THE
## POST-BRAIN SURGERY
## JOURNALS

# Louise Krug

*Louise Krug*

99: THE PRESS
San Francisco, CA and Lowell, MA
2016

"The real voyage of discovery consists not in seeking new landscapes, but in having new eyes."

—**Marcel Proust**, *Remembrance of Things Past*

"The body is our general medium for having a world."

—**Maurice Merleau-Ponty**, *Phenomenology of Perception*

"It was easy for me to ascribe to physical beauty certain qualities that I thought I simply had to wait for. It was easier to think that I was still not beautiful enough or lovable enough than to admit that perhaps these qualities did not really belong to this thing I thought was called beauty after all."

—**Lucy Grealy**, *Autobiography of a Face*

# Table of Contents

*For Nick*

# Introduction

In 2006, at age 22, I had two craniotomies to remove a cavernous angioma from my brainstem. A cavernous angioma is a mass of malformed blood vessels, and mine was round and red. It looked like a raspberry. The surgeries (there were two because the first was unsuccessful) removed the possibility of the angioma's further bleeding, but also changed me as I knew myself. Because of the damage the surgeries caused to various cranial nerves, my left eye turned permanently towards my nose, causing double vision, and the left side of my face was paralyzed, making it difficult to speak and eat. The right side of my body lost enough feeling and coordination that normal activities such as walking and bathing—really, any physical activity—became difficult. I had to learn a new way of living. While several subsequent surgeries on my face and eye have alleviated some circumstances a bit—implanting a gold weight in my left eyelid means I can close it; splicing together some facial nerves means that if I press the tip of my tongue to the roof of my mouth, the left side of my face can form a simulation of a smile—I am still learning.

The procedures altered everything. Instead of soaking up Southern California sun, dating a Frenchman, and pursuing a career in tabloid journalism, I moved back to Kansas, went to graduate school, married a Missouri guy, and had two children. I didn't "get better" so much as I adjusted. This book is less about the *cure* and more about the *adjustment*.

Most of the pieces in this book take place over a period of five years, from around 2009 to 2014. As a writer, I'm interested not merely in telling stories about my experiences but in reflecting on the ways in which I told stories to myself in order to make sense of the experience. Just as the procedures left me with a kind of doubleness, so, too, is there a doubleness of narrative and experience—the narratives we weave in real time during the experience itself and the ones we revisit later that comprise a book.

I tell my stories in the third person because it comes easiest to me, maybe because I really do *see* differently now. I will make no claim that I wouldn't trade my body now for the one I had pre-surgery because I've learned so much or grown as a human being. I will, admit, though, that because of the course my life has taken, I may have become a different person than I might otherwise have been—more grateful, perhaps, more thankful for the health I now enjoy, and in Kansas, no less, the very place I never pictured myself living.

My life now is tilted: changed from what it had been, a bit skewed, but still mine. I see, say, two cups of coffee where in reality there is only one, and they seem to bounce up and down (the nystagmus, a vision disorder caused by the surgeries). But I have learned to only reach for only one of the cups, and I understand that it is sitting still on the table. By now, I know things are not what they look like. They are more.

# What Do You Want to Remember?

Louise didn't want a wedding photographer.

She wanted all the rest of getting married: the sparkly ring, the lacy dress that rustled and trailed a train. She wanted Pachelbel's Canon in D, Rilke poems, champagne toasts and a towering buttercream-frosted cake. She wanted a gauzy veil and a honeymoon on an island, a bachelorette party complete with ten girlfriends all making drunken confessions in a limousine. If she didn't look at herself, she could imagine she was any other woman getting married. It was her turn.

But photos would ruin it.

She told Nick as much in the car on their way to meet a potential photographer, because of course they had to get a photographer. There had to be pictures. They had attended a wedding where the DJ never showed and the groom had to hook his phone up to the speakers for some music. They had been to weddings with plastic flowers, weddings with no alcohol, one in a sweltering wheat field, and another in a courthouse basement with fluorescent lighting. But they had never been to a wedding where there was no photographer.

"It'll be fine, trust me," said Nick, as they pulled up to the photographer's house. Being a photographer himself, for a newspaper, he was familiar with Louise's neuroses with photos. It pained him to see how much she disliked looking at herself. He understood it, sort of, except that he had only known Louise after her surgeries, had fallen in love with her face lopsided and all, however far from perfect it was. They had met two years ago, and at first she never let him take photos of her—not that he asked much, knowing she hated it. Now she was better, less resistant to being captured digitally. But wedding photos were on an entirely different level.

"I'll be the ugly bride," she'd say when he brought it up. All he could ever do was shake his head.

✶

Much of the wedding experience had been hard for Louise. Finding a dress, for instance. It was complicated, because she loved the idea of going shopping for one with her mother, Janet. They would go into a bridal store and scour the aisles of giant clear garment bags. Ball gowns, mermaids, and slip-like sheaths, some with tiny details like gold thread or seed pearls, some nothing but seemingly endless yards of gleaming satin. Janet handed Louise dress after dress over the changing room curtain, and when Louise slowly emerged, her shoulders always caved in.

"You look perfect!" Janet said each time, always followed by "What, what is it?"

Louise would stand in front of the three-way mirror on a little carpeted pedestal so that the gown could be seen in its full glory.

"I just never look how I think I will. I just . . ." and then Louise would trail off and look at the girl in the next dressing booth, smiling at her reflection.

"Oh sweetie, I know," Janet would say.

But she didn't know.

*

Louise finally found a dress, and a veil, and shoes. She found a wish jar (a giant glass vase for guests to put their hopes for the newlyweds on scraps of paper) and had Nick make table-seating card-holders out of wine corks with a razor blade. She found a bird-cage for the gift cards and had her father draw and photocopy a custom map for all the guests. She had meeting after meeting with the flower people, the cake lady, and the caterer. And she loved it all, except thinking about the photographer.

*

Louise had been a bridesmaid in four girlfriends' weddings since her surgeries. One of the weddings had been in an old opera house in a small town in central Kansas, two had been close to Lake Michigan, and one on a golf course—well, until it rained at the last minute, and it was moved to the clubhouse next to the golf course. For Louise, the picture-taking was always the uncomfortable part. With the wedding party standing in unnatural formations around the bride and groom, Louise could feel the photographer singling her out as strange-looking, mentally shrugging before getting on with the required shots.

But Janet's wedding a few years ago to her second husband, the Doctor, and only 18 months out from the surgeries, had been the worst. During that photo shoot Grammy, Janet's mom, called the shots. After the ceremony, everybody was at the front of the church by the altar for a big family portrait, and Louise was standing next to Janet, holding a bouquet of white tulips and wearing a mushroom-colored shift. Grammy kept going to the photographer and shouting things to the group, telling Louise's brothers to smooth their hair and Janet to put on more lipstick.

"Oh, mother," Janet kept saying. She wore a knee-length, ivory skirt-suit that Louise had said was "very Jackie O."

And then she zeroed in on Louise.

"Something just doesn't look right," Louise's grandmother kept saying to the photographer as she looked at the tiny images on his camera.

"Louise, smile more, or maybe tilt your head?" she went on. "Weezy, can you look at the camera more straight on?" Grammy called out, using her hands as a megaphone.

It was then, in front of her brothers, her mother the bride, and her grandmother, that Louise began to cry.

It caused a scene.

Janet had to comfort Louise in the church bathroom, and the guests had to wait an extra half hour for them to show up at the reception hall. The final result that hung on Janet and the Doctor's living-room wall showed Louise standing, bleary, feet just a bit too spaced for balance, with white knuckles around her bouquet. Louise wished Janet would take it down.

✳

This all could have been avoided, just as Louise's impending wedding photo shoot could be avoided. What if there was no big wedding? What if Louise and Nick got married in, say, their back yard on a Tuesday and then went out for martinis? What if they got married at a barbecue in matching white T-shirts, or on an Alaskan cruise? Why did Louise feel it had to be a certain way?

She really wanted that wedding album, damn it. She wanted a picture on her living-room wall, too. She wanted normal because she was not. And so she found herself in a situation she had been in many times since the surgeries, though perhaps not to this degree, where she found herself both wanting and not wanting the same thing. She wanted documentary evidence of what would certainly be among the happiest days of her life, a day that, in her bleakest moments, she feared might never happen. But now, it was happening. And she wondered what was worse: to have no pictures of her dreamed-of day, or to have images of that dream with her self-conscious pose, her slightly paralyzed face, her posture less elegantly poised and more rigidly balanced. Would she choose not to mark the day or to have the day doubly marked?

*

She got out of the car at the photographer's house. She walked in through the door. She sat down with her fiancée. She was thinking about not crying and acting excited. Because she would be, right? If she were anyone else. At least twice, she almost turned around and went back out the door. But she stayed.

In her conversation with the wedding photographer, Louise requested that he shoot only her face's good side. That was the side that moved. The photographer said no problem, easy peasy. He acted as if he didn't even notice anything different with Louise's face, barely looked her in the eye. Louise liked it better when doctors and plastic surgeons scrutinized her, took her head in their hands and gently turned it this way and that, looking at her from different angles. She felt a relief in that. In being seen for what she was. One wall of the photographer's basement studio was covered with framed wedding portraits he had shot: the peaceful bride with a small smile looking out a window, a grinning groom dipping his chosen one in a corn field while the sun set, her teeth glowing in

7

her upside-down face. Even the photos that captured the brides dancing at the reception—their hair a little limp and their lipstick sweated off, their silly movements forever frozen in time, clutching a beer bottle—even those brides had what Louise wanted: complete and utter existence in the moment, total embodiment of the experience. Unselfconscious joy. She wondered whether the photographer would put her photograph on his wall. Could he make her look normal? Bride-like? She didn't expect miracles, or maybe she did. The meeting didn't last long, and except for her request of shooting her on her good side, she let Nick do most of the talking. After leaving the photographer's house she felt better, or maybe it was resigned. But on the wedding day Louise was still dreading him showing up.

In the end, though, it wasn't that bad. This time, it was Louise in the center of the cheesy wedding party poses, her bridesmaids in yellow tulle that they would never wear again. The photographer shot Louise, Nick, and the wedding party walking across the street from the hotel where they got married, everyone acting relaxed and attempting candid motions, like actors when they're offstage. This made her reflect on how her anxieties affected her actual enjoyment of the event itself. She wondered whether she would be plagued with this burden of an advanced reading of her life.

After it was all over, was Louise happy with how the photos turned out? Well, she liked the pictures that made her look thin, the ones where her eyes looked aligned and her mouth was a straight line. But there were others, too, that pleased her. There was a shot of Nick, laughing at some slipup she made during her vows. She liked that one. She liked one of her and Nick arm in arm, walking down the aisle of the hotel ballroom after the ceremony, almost running, really. They looked relieved, and they were looking at someone out of the frame, someone they recognized. Nick was waving. They looked like they knew, even then, that this would not be the best day of their lives. They look like they were saying goodbye to the whole wedding experience, like they were heading outside to their car, and then they were going to drive all the way to Mexico. There, on their honeymoon, was where the best days would start. Start, and stop. Start, and stop. All the days of their lives.

"What served in place of the photograph, before
the camera's invention? The expected answer is
the engraving, the drawing, the painting. The more
revealing answer might be: memory. What photographs
do out there was previously done within reflection...
Memory implies a certain act of redemption. What
is remembered has been saved from nothingness.
What is forgotten has been abandoned."

—**John Berger**, "Uses of Photography"



"Life is not about significant details, illuminated
a flash, a fixed forever. Photographs are."

—**Susan Sontag**, *On Photography*

# Where Do You Live?

One was listed as a fifties designer style. The ceilings were low pop-corn, the floors all linoleum, and the bathrooms painted in garish pink. Louise had thought they could make it work until Nick glee-fully came upon a collapsed retaining wall in the backyard.

"One hard rain would wash us all away," he said. The other house they saw, a rambler, was across the street from a cemetery.

Inside the newest pick, a brown bungalow, they pictured them-selves with the furniture, photos, and books they owned already, as well as the many things they would have to buy.

"Like a real kitchen table," Nick said. "No more eating dinner on the couch."

"Or a chandelier." Louise said, mostly serious. Nick and Louise were currently living in a rental whose washing machine was on the porch. Their landlady did things like show up on Saturday mornings to rip ivy off the side of the house because it was a parasite. They wanted a house with walls they could paint celery green, with no upstairs neighbors who wore boots and stomped around or cooked dinners that had fishy smells. They wanted to own a place where they could say "our house" and mean it. Louise was still in graduate school and Nick at the newspaper so they couldn't afford much, but something was better than nothing. In short, Louise wanted normalcy. After three years of the abnormal, and after being forced to rethink and re-evaluate her sense of what *normal* might mean, she wanted something that might line up with what others might also see as *normal*.

The seller appeared in the kitchen. He had a red pointy beard and crazy jeans, the kind that make men look like they have hips. He was not supposed to be there, the realtor said.

"I've been working in my wood shop in the basement," he said. "Gotta make a living, right?" He laughed loudly.

"O.K.," the realtor said.

The seller looked angry. "Listen," he said, "I don't know. Do you people even know how to care for the wood counter-tops in the kitchen? These can't be sprayed with some shitty cleanser, they need a special kind you have to order on the Internet."

The realtor held up her hand.

Louise knew that someone else lived in the house; all home buyers understand this. But at the looking stage, the pre-buying stage, all potential home owners like to imagine the house they could move into as a kind of tabula rasa. Louise was prepared to encounter human items like dishes and appliances and even artifacts that revealed the taste of the owner (who she preferred to remain imaginary and anonymous), but she was not prepared to have to encounter the owner himself. She did not want to put a face to a place.

Louise was opening the kitchen cabinets. They were wooden, painted white, with little chrome pulls. She was opening each and every one.

"I made those," the seller said.

He said he had gutted the kitchen and all of this was his. "I have pictures," he said, pulling a photo album off a shelf. The realtor took the album from the seller and set it on the counter. Louise tried to pull a bottom drawer open and it wouldn't budge. She planted both feet on the floor and Nick held her waist and she strained, but the drawer still did nothing.

"Hey," she said to the realtor, "make a note of this."

"No!" the seller said, shooing Louise out of the way. "You just have to give it a good tug."

They watched as he pulled, purple in the face.

They moved on to the bedroom. "The only issue here is that this bedroom is not really a bedroom," the realtor said.

"What are you talking about, there's a bed right here," the seller said, and flopped down on his belly. The quilt was covered in roses.

"No closets," Louise said, remembering something she had learned from *House Buying 101*. "So it doesn't really count."

"That doesn't actually matter, does it?" Nick said, looking at Louise with his chin pointing up. The realtor shrugged.

"I don't make the rules," she said.

"Let's see the basement," Nick said. He had been saying during the whole house-hunting process that the basement was the key. "If the basement is good, we're golden," he always said. It had to be dry. No cracks in the walls. He kept talking about all the storage possibilities, like shelves for Christmas lights and canned food.

As they trudged down the wooden basement stairs, they left the seller walking around the kitchen, opening little drawers and making a snack.

"Have a good look," he said. "It will have more room than you ever need."

*

Nick and Louise were in a hurry about this house thing, especially Louise—so much so that they went to meet their realtor pretty late at night, long after they had gotten home from work and eaten sandwiches and when they would normally be watching a T.V. show. The way Louise understood it, once you had a house, you were somewhere. And she needed to feel somewhere permanent. She had met Nick after she had moved back to Kansas again, after her brain surgeries. She looked different, walked different, and knew that everyone saw her differently too. Nick was her guy, she had no doubt: he ate her burned tofu, unclogged the toilet in the same bathroom where he killed all the spiders, and spooned her all night long. But it wasn't enough. She wanted to feel like she was where she was supposed to be. She wanted to feel home. So they bought this one because it seemed like a house where they could live an ordinary life. It had a little front porch painted periwinkle and begging for a swing, and a redbud tree in the front yard that somewhat blocked the shabby house across the street with the smiley face mailbox. Big windows bathed the house in light, and although it had a basic bathroom and a single closet, it charmed her with its wood floors and built-in bookshelves. The best spot was the airy kitchen, which the seller had painted the color of butter. The countertops were dark, rich walnut, sanded and stained. You could stay in there all day, Louise thought. That was what they needed. A place they could stay.

When Nick and Louise arrived with the first truckload of boxes on move-in day, the seller and his family were far from gone. As Louise scrubbed out the sticky refrigerator, the seller and another man moved saws, sanders, and other equipment up from his basement wood shop. As Nick brought in box after box he made chitchat with the wife, who seemed timid and kind. She was a medical transcriptionist and worked out of the single room upstairs, which was a meager office with no heating or cooling. The children, ages five and eight, ran around hugging doorways and lying spread-eagle on the floor, saying "Bye house! We love you!" Though white Midwesterners, they were named Native American names, one meaning "jester" and the other "wings." The family was moving to Colorado, pursuing a dream and joining friends who had made the move years earlier. After they had finally driven off in late afternoon, Louise and Nick discovered they had forgotten to leave the house keys. They called the seller on his cell phone and met him at a nearby grocery store. A week later Nick called the wife because the two couches they had left on the porch for "friends to pick up" were still there. While Nick was explaining this to the wife he heard the seller in the background say "Too bad, it's your problem now!" Strangely, Louise and Nick felt connected to the couple. One of the times they had toured the house before buying it, they had seen a tube of Astroglide beside their bed. Their own bed was now in that same place, and they drifted off to sleep looking out the same window at night. They constantly found reminders of the family around the house: plastic army men in the hostas, comic strips taped to a basement wall, poorly painted corners. Louise couldn't help but wonder how this house would shape her and Nick. Who would they turn into?

*

People on their new street were friendly, so far. There were Brenè and Toni, the lesbian couple who had an adopted daughter and maintained a meticulous yard. There was Mrs. Shepherd across the street, who was very old and came out once a day to get the mail. And there was Mike from two houses down, who lived with his elderly, legally blind father and two big, black dogs. They first met Mike a week after they moved in. It was a Sunday, midafternoon, and they were working hard, hanging up pictures and stacking books into shelves. Louise answered the door and there stood Mike, fifty years old, gas-station sunglasses, a loose mouth of wild teeth, and a head that was mostly shaved with a long ponytail on top. He was standing in the doorway with his legs wide apart, holding a paper plate covered in foil, which he thrust toward Louise.

"Pierogies," he said. "I made them myself. Just stuffed crescent rolls with cabbage and cooked them in the Fry Daddy."

This was exactly the sort of thing that Louise had hoped would happen after moving into their house. She made meaningful eye contact with Nick, who went to the fridge for beer for them all, and invited Mike in to sit down. They found out a lot about Mike: he had to been to jail for theft and was a mechanic. His garage was his "sanctuary" and he had a couple of ex-wives. His dad annoyed the shit out of him and shouldn't drive, but did, using a monocle.

"Oh, I've seen him," Nick said.

Mike saw himself as the neighborhood watchdog. After about an hour, he stood up and said,

"You have any problems with anyone, you come to me."

Then he was gone.

Mike's visits started to become regular, usually on Sundays in the late afternoon when Louise and Nick were raking leaves in the front yard or unloading the car from a trip to the grocery store. Mike brought over vegetables from his garden in plastic bags: three heads of cabbage, onions, carrots. Louise was touched, and when she made a big pot of spaghetti sauce she sent Nick to his house with a container.

They got used to hearing Mike blasting country music out of his garage while working on his car with his shirt off even in cold weather, and if they were driving home from a movie late at night, they would see him and his dad walking their dogs on the side of the road, holding flashlights, those big black dogs silent, never barking, not once.

One Sunday afternoon, Nick had run to the hardware store and Mike knocked on the door. Louise made a point of making them both cups of tea. By now she could tell that Mike had a drinking problem by his belches and smell—vodka *did* have a smell, she thought.

"Hey, I have to ask you something," Mike said, pushing the cup of tea away before he tried it.

"Sure," Louise said. She thought maybe he would confide in her about women problems, and that made her nervous. She couldn't imagine that she would have any advice to give.

"What happened to your eye?" he said. "Why does it turn in like that?"

Louise felt like she'd been tricked. She said, "Oh," and told Mike about the brain surgeries, the term "cavernous angioma," and talked about her special glasses, which he asked to see.

"Wow, these are pretty nuts," he said, trying on her thick glasses with the special prism lens, his oily, melon-like head stretching the frames. Louise winced. He handed the glasses back, yawned.

"Your situation kind of reminds me about these dental problems I had a few years back," he said, scooching back his chair and heading for the door. "Endless trips to Kansas City. Horrible doctors. Hang in there, my friend." He shut the door.

Louise felt like he'd caught her undressing or going to the bathroom. She was always taken by surprise when someone asked her about her eye or face. There would be months of nothing, and then the cashier at the grocery store would ask if she had Bell's palsy, or a fellow campus bus passenger would ask if it was Parkinson's. Louise would be going along, living her life, thinking about what she was going to cook with that chicken in the fridge or if she could make herself do a yoga DVD before dinner and then, bam, someone would remind her that she was different. She usually gave the questioner a dry, abridged explanation just complicated enough that they wouldn't be able to ask any more questions. But why was it so bad to be different? Louise didn't know. She suspected it had something to do with her traditional ideal of beauty, and the way that she didn't fit into it anymore. But she had Nick, and he loved her, and told her she was beautiful all the time. Why wasn't that enough?

It wasn't enough because Nick wasn't the only person she saw every day. It helped, of course, that he made her feel good, but he wasn't the only person she was making an impression on. She also had classmates, students, professors of her own that she had to deal with as well as random strangers. She couldn't shake why she cared if they thought she was pretty. It had to do with your body being who you are, and she didn't see how she would ever get away from that idea. Since she was a little girl, how she looked was a part of who she was. That was in her, and it was never going to go away, not even when she needed it to.

Things changed with Mike after that. Louise didn't eat his pierogies anymore, just put them in the trash when he left. Nick started talking to him on the porch instead of inviting him in. Mike's visits became more and more infrequent, probably because he sensed their coldness. Louise had been excited to make all the neighbors Christmas cookies, had bought special tins at the Dollar Store and had a recipe picked out, but squashed the idea as the holiday got closer.

Louise realized she may have overreacted to Mike's questioning. He didn't mean to be rude. Perhaps by then in their relationship he felt he had earned her trust enough to be able to satisfy his curiosity and that in return they would become even closer. But, still, the fact that she had reacted the way she did, and did so every time anyone, even a child, commented on her differences, told her something: she wasn't comfortable with herself, even after what she felt a long time had passed since the surgeries. Even after meeting Nick, falling in love, and getting married. Even after making good friends, going to graduate school, and buying a house. None of it mattered. She might as well have had the brain surgeries yesterday—that's how ill-fitting this new body felt sometimes. She wanted to know *when*. When would people's questions stop being upsetting? When would she be able to explain, in a genial tone, what happened to her eye or face, and not give it a second thought after the person nodded, smiled quickly, and went away. When would that be? It bothered Louise that things were fine with her odd neighbor as long as he did not ask her about her eye, as long as he was the weird one. But, as soon as that relationship inverted, as soon as the ex-con alcoholic twice-divorced man made a comparison with her by way of a *defect*, it shifted everything—how she saw him, but more importantly how she suddenly realized he saw her.

One night she and Nick were sitting on their couch, drinking wine and getting ready to watch a documentary Louise had heard about. Louise stretched. "I don't care about being neighborly anymore, knowing anyone on our street, smiling and waving or anything. We have our house, it's enough," she said.

"O.K.," Nick said. "But just because some of our neighbors are weird doesn't mean we can't be friends with any of them." He drank the last his of his wine. "Like what about Brenè and Toni? They're so nice to us."

Louise snorted. "All right. Maybe I'll make them some cookies. But that's it." She pulled a kitchen chair over to the couch and set up her computer so they could watch the movie on it.

The documentary was about dolphin poaching in Japan, an unnecessary and hateful practice. Louise and Nick also had seen documentaries about:

Expensive, elite preschools in New York City.

Chinese parents who left their homes to work far away in factories and never saw their children.

A wealthy time-share king, his sexy, dumb wife, their six kids, and how they lost it all.

An autistic artist.

A woman who said she was a child-painter prodigy on Facebook and got away with it, for a while.

A big-time country singer who came out as a lesbian.

A sexual-abuse scandal in the suburbs.

A chef.

All the documentaries told stories about lives destroyed. All told stories about loss, and some showed hope. All included emotions as mild as disappointment, embarrassment, of wishing life was different. All showed a moving on.

In the documentary that was Louise's life, the question remained—would Louise move on, or would she mire?

"That image, of the self, does not belong equally to everyone. As a woman, I must keep myself under constant surveillance: how do I look as I rise from the bed, and when I walk through the store buying groceries, and while I run with the dog in the park? From childhood I was taught to survey and police and maintain my image continually, and in this role—as both surveyor and the image that is surveyed—I learned to see myself as others see me: as an object to be viewed and evaluated, a sight."

—**Lacy M. Johnson**, *The Other Side: A Memoir*

# Dress For the Job You Want

Louise could never decide what to wear for teaching. Should she wear the navy blouse made out of shiny cotton sateen? It had a scoop neck and brown appliqué polka dots around the collar and cap sleeves. She had spent a lot of money on it, ordering it from a British company that took ten days to deliver. The model on the website tossed a head of glossy waves and laughed while holding a latte—that was what Louise was going for. She had bought so many "teacher" clothes: a red-and-white patterned shell (one student, in her course evaluation, said it looked like a crossword puzzle), periwinkle velvet wide-legged trousers, and a jersey dress that reminded Louise of the jolly green giant because of its brown and green print. There was the cream-colored linen skirt with cornflower swirls, a corduroy blazer, a sweater dress. If asked, she wouldn't be able to define "teacher" clothes articulately; she only knew that they were conservative without being uptight, grown-up without being old, fun without being zany. In short, they were how she wanted to be as a teacher. She wanted the clothes to guide her.

Louise thought of how often she looked at her own teachers, daydreaming about their personal lives when she was supposed to be listening: Who was in love with these professors? What did they eat for lunch? What faces did they make when they were alone? There was the young, classically beautiful literature teacher who wore black wool turtlenecks in July, the stylish writing instructor with a big diamond and biker jacket, and the old man advisor with a white ponytail and turquoise belt buckle. Louise didn't know what her students imagined about her, but she wanted to try to make it better than her actual life. More interesting. She knew that her face would always be off-kilter, that her best smile would be forced, having to remember to push her tongue up against the back of her teeth. Because of the partial paralysis, only one side of her face could respond to a funny remark, creating a lopsided look. But maybe the right clothes could make up for it. Or at least distract. A student might think, "Weird-looking face, but always put-together and frequent haircuts." That would be O.K.

The hardest part of dressing like a teacher was the shoes. Due to half her body being weak, balance was a problem and when she walked, her right foot dragged slightly. Heels were out as well as anything that didn't completely encase her foot, including ballerinas or sexy sling-backs. Louise tended to buy shoes from online stores like FootSmart and Cushe, always in the hope of finding a slightly sexy, supportive, multiple-strapped, flat style. (They don't exist.)

Jaqui, one of her closest friends in her teaching training program, was beautiful, truly one of the most physically perfect women Louise had ever seen. To teach, Jaqui always wore: leggings and white T-shirts. Flip-flops even when it snowed. It didn't matter. Her ancestry was half white American, half Saudi Arabian, with boobs and a butt and dark brown hair that waved down to the middle of her back. The kind of eyebrows you saw in old movies. Jaqui could actually wear kohl eyeliner, or big hoop earrings, things that would make Louise look like she was dressing up for Halloween. Jaqui's students loved her, not only because they never tired of looking at her but because she was smart and funny. She was a great writer, too, with essays about her tumultuous relationship with her mother and her complicated, tragic family at large.

Louise got to know Jaqui in a graduate writing workshop. Jaqui would always get there late, with a soda and chips from the vending machine in hand, and would sit at the far end of the long oval table with one leg tucked under her, commenting on whatever anyone was saying. Louise was annoyed with her at first—Louise, who always got to school early and brought a travel mug of tea to class, who went to bed by 10 p.m. even on weekends and never needed an alarm. But Jaqui was irresistible—and she and Louise soon began having drinks at a fancy bar downtown where Jaqui's boyfriend worked. They drank Prosecco or vodka gimlets, and in the dim lighting and against a backdrop of abstract art that went up, up, up to the high ceilings of the building that was once a bank, they talked about teaching.

"I got an email from a student who hasn't been to class in weeks wanting to know what the homework was," said Jaqui, reaching over to push a chunk of hair out of Louise's eyes.

"What did you tell him?" Louise said.

"Nothing. I don't answer emails like that," Jaqui said. Louise loved that. She was always afraid that if she were to do something similar she would destroy her "nice teacher" persona, which was the one thing she thought she had going for her. They talked about confiscating their students' phones in class, or their students' silly writing mistakes ("you're vs. your," "in society today," etc.). They talked about the drudgery of grading and planning and the temptation to just wing a class, but of course they never did.

Louise admired Jaqui for her guts with students, how she would fail them after a certain number of absences (something Louise only threatened to do), and envied her for the way students, especially female ones, would come by her office and confide personal problems to her. They always left sniffling but smiling. They never graded together, as Jaqui was the type to stay up all night, fueled by caffeine, and blaze through twenty-two papers, while Louise diligently did four a day until the stack was done.

They never talked about Jaqui's physical beauty. There was nothing to say, it was obvious. If they ever needed a table at a restaurant or had a question for a salesperson, Jaqui was always the one who asked. People reacted to her differently; that was just how it was. And after a while Louise forgot how beautiful Jaqui was—she was just Jaqui—but then she would remember all over again when they would meet someone new, guy or girl, and the person would pull Louise aside to say, "so this Jaqui . . . ."

A funny thing about Jaqui and Louise's friendship was that Jaqui would always comment on how Louise looked. "You always have such perfect hair," she would say to Louise, or "You always look put-together. When do you look sloppy?" Louise, who blew-dry her shoulder-length, blonde-highlighted hair the same way every day and wore mostly jeans and solid-color T-shirts, was tickled that Jaqui saw her this way. Jaqui built up her confidence, made her forget she was trying to be a teacher and made her feel like a regular girlfriend. A put-together girlfriend at that.

Jacqui moved to South Carolina for a writing fellowship that summer, and although they stayed friends for a while, it wasn't the same as being together all the time. Louise was left with a ragged feeling of wondering what had been real about their friendship, and afraid that she would never know.

*

After college, Louise had moved to Southern California with her French boyfriend. Set up in a tiny apartment in a village called Summerland, just south of Santa Barbara, she freelanced for a brief time before she got sick. She wrote about paper shredders for *Santa Barbara Business Journal* and covered Britney Spears for *US Weekly*. Reporting was a balancing act: finding the right sources, reeling them in, and establishing a rapport. She had loved it. She had worked for the college newspaper since she was eighteen, thriving on the camaraderie among the staff and the euphoria of meeting a deadline. In her heart, however, Louise wasn't a serious journalist. In her mind, the local election results were equal to a successful pancake feed, which was equal to an interview with the superintendent. Maybe she should have seen this indifference as a bad sign, a hint that she should try a different career, but she didn't.

After the brain surgeries, though, journalism lost its appeal. The task of seeking a story, talking to new people, day after day, was the last thing she wanted to do. She needed to find a way of life where she could exist, if not escape, inside her head, and not have to confront strangers for a living. So she chose to go back to graduate school and get an MFA in creative writing. Her brain surgeries were easy fodder: crawling on the hospital floor with her physical therapist, learning to walk again after the surgeries; being too self-conscious about her eyes to take the trash out at her apartment building without sunglasses. At first, in workshops, she disguised herself in fictional characters, but soon she moved into memoir.

Teaching, the part of grad school that paid her tuition, was entirely different from writing, however. Teaching was nothing but interacting with people, nothing but allowing yourself to be scrutinized and quite possibly disliked. Her students, usually first-year undergraduates, eighteen and nineteen years old, had been involved with the teacher-versus-student dynamic most of their lives. No, teaching didn't make sense for Louise, because it meant opening herself up to so many critiques, so many chances for meanness, or if not meanness, then simply to examination. None of her students had ever said anything to her about her eye or face, but Louise was always waiting for it. Fortunately, even when she was sitting one-on-one with a student in her office, laughing at something together, that invisible buffer of the word "teacher" seemed to always stop the hanging question, "What happened to your face?" Maybe being a teacher, someone who was always supposed to be separate from her students, different, was the best job she could hope for, in terms of always keeping a little bit of protective distance, always being able to turn away. Louise felt best when she was teaching a writing workshop. She knew how to be encouraging, how to talk about point of view, or dialogue, or setting. She knew how to steer an unproductive discussion ("but it really happened like this!") onto some sort of productive path. She felt especially lucky when choosing which books the class would read during the semester—what better life than this?

She felt the worst when teaching a composition class and trying to convince the students that writing a paper about ethos, pathos, and logos was crucial to their career path, or, say, explaining the relevance of a passage in their textbooks from the 1980s. It was hard to get excited about showing the class a pristine Works Cited page on the overhead projector or reading the umpteenth paper aimed at persuading her that marijuana was not a gateway drug.

No, something in a cubicle, with a computer and a headset, might have been a more obvious choice for someone who was so insecure. When Louise was first out of the hospital she had daydreams about becoming a receptionist at the Mayo Clinic, where she had undergone her surgeries, and marrying a doctor. They would have a little apartment, and she would be there every night when he came home. Sort of a reverse Florence Nightingale effect.

There was something about how her doctors cared for her, looked out for her, and knew what was best for her that made her want to never leave their care. They had held her life in her hands and they had saved her, so whom else did she need? Who was more attractive than a doctor, for those very reasons? What else was there in life?

*

Somehow, Louise's ability to stand in front of a classroom was connected to her identity as a writer. Since she had starting writing, she felt more comfortable in that writer-skin than in one simply as a woman. Her appearance didn't need to please others. That wasn't her job. Maybe because being a writer, for her, anyway, had nothing to do with the way you looked, or what you even thought of yourself. Your identity was your work: if you were a writer, then that was what you were. Nothing else mattered. If that was true, though, then why did Louise care one bit about the way she looked? Why didn't she show up to teach in the same black pants and blue shirt every day, the way one of her friends in her program had? It had been a man who had done this, actually; a very good writer who really didn't care about what he looked like (though he was very handsome in a peaked sort of way). His students had complained about his wearing the same clothes day after day on his evaluations, which he had found amusing, but he was also mystified as to why they would care. Louise, however, was not. How you dressed for your students, who were in a sense your audience, did matter to them. They wanted to know that you cared, even if your way of caring was strange to them.

# Janet's Clothes

Janet, Louise's mother, had started wearing her own mother's old clothes. They all called Janet's mother Grammy.

"See, she was the same height as me, but much wider," she said to Louise, bunching in her fist the back of a plaid wool jacket, or maybe a mink coat. Janet wore Grammy's blazers with shoulder pads and gold-braid detail to work, and had even gotten into the costume jewelry, like coral necklaces or rings with big black stones. Janet and Grammy had the same shoe size, too, so in the winter Janet went around in some white fur boots with brass toes. In the springtime she started appearing in some dirty cork sandals.

Grammy had died unexpectedly. She fell to the floor early one morning as she was standing before her closet deciding what to wear. Granddad was only 10 feet away brushing his teeth. His back was turned toward her. When he turned around, she was dead.

She was 77. Louise had been 28 at the time.

Janet and Louise saw each other often because they lived close by—Janet's small town was about an hour away from Louise's college hub. Once a week or so, they would be together in a car, going to an outlet mall in search of new khakis, when a certain type of talk would start. Janet would be remembering Grammy's oddities, and Louise would sit up straighter.

"She used to write checks for five dollars instead of using cash! And she always had to be at the church the day after Christmas, picking up trash in the parking lot. Once, she cleaned the pews with furniture polish, remember?"

"She stayed with me for two weeks each time after you and your brothers were born," Janet said, she driving and Louise in the passenger's seat. "I cried so hard each time she left."

Louise joined in.

"Remember her St. Patrick's Day parties?" Louise said. "That one year, when I had my eye patch, how she made me put on a green plastic bowler hat and serve Irish coffee to her friends? And what about the way she killed snakes? With a hoe."

It was true. When Louise had been waiting to hear where she would have brain surgery she stayed at Janet's, and Grammy often kept her company.

One day, Janet and Louise sat at a tiny table in a mezzanine, trying not to spill their coffee. It was a Saturday, and they were at a trade show, looking for possible choices for Janet's kitchen counters, which she was redoing. Louise liked helping with those things. She and Nick were fixing up their new house, too. They painted walls colors like Crème Brûlée, or Russian Blue. They bought furniture on Craigslist, which meant they had to meet the sellers in parking lots because no one wanted a stranger to know where they lived.

"I have a surprise for you," Janet said, giving Louise a heavy paper sack. "Wait until you get home to look."

Janet had on a baggy red silk blouse with a ruffled collar and putty-colored pants; both had been Grammy's. The pants sagged in the bottom and were of a thick cloth that was somehow spongy. Despite this she was still beautiful. Growing up, Louise's friends had always called Janet "the pretty mom." Her brown bob was shiny, her olive skin still smooth. Louise looked like Janet, people said, but Louise didn't see it. They had the same round face, the same quick smile. The same small hands and feet, long legs and arms. But Louise's hair was lighter in color, and further highlighted blonde. She had blue eyes where Janet had hazel, and Janet was much more petite than Louise, who was on the tall side and wore a size 8. Louise had often wondered about her body, about her physicality. She was 5'8", weighed roughly 140 pounds. Before her surgeries she would have thought her best features were her eyes and her smile, but now she thought they were her worst; her shoulders now were her best, she thought. Before her surgeries she would have thought of herself as "pretty," and she assumed some percentage of others (maybe 50–60%) would have thought so as well. Had she been "hot?" Was she "sexy?" She thought so, but she wasn't sure, and she really had no idea if men thought those things when they saw her back then. After her surgeries, she was even more uncertain about her prettiness. Would people notice her eye? Would that trump her height? Would her wit override concerns about her eye? Lop-sided smile? It did with Nick, but she wondered sometimes about him and what Nick told himself about her eye. Did he ever notice it? Daily? Weekly? Hourly?

"I have to get going," Janet said, rooting around in her purse for her keys. "Duty calls." Janet was going to cook a special dinner tonight for her father, the Grandfather. He had lived with Janet and the Doctor since the day after Grammy died. It was he who had advised Janet to wear her mother's clothes. "For goodness sake, no sense in letting them go to waste," he'd said. "Those are very fine items. Perfectly good."

When she got home, Louise emptied the bag on her bed. It was nothing but stretched-out sports bras in colors like hot pink and purple and long, loose nightgowns with eyelet lace on the sleeves. Grammy's. Louise thought about wearing them, tried them on.

Louise remembered her grandmother in those nightgowns, entering the kitchen in late morning during Louise's visits, frowzy with sleep. Grammy usually slept late because she had trouble sleeping at night, and she would lie in bed and listen to satellite public radio shows on headphones at 3 a.m. Subsequently, Grammy was constantly spouting off stories she had heard the night before. One morning, over coffee and cinnamon rolls, she might inform Louise on the right way to wash raw chicken, the history of tortellini (the dumpling inspired by Venus' navel), and the latest outbreak of the Dengue fever in Florida. Grammy had silver hair, pink skin, and eyes like water. Janet bore some resemblance to her, but Louise looked nothing like her. She was someone else.

*

Sometimes, Janet would talk about conversations she had with Grammy that she wished she could take back.

"About once a week," she said to Louise, "Mom would come over to the house without calling first, just to say hi. I would get so annoyed. I'd be busy! She didn't work. She had nowhere to be. I was impatient. I was sometimes rude."

Louise and Janet were at a clothing store, the kind that sold endless varieties of blue jeans. Janet had a weakness for finding the perfect pair, and when Louise went on the hunt with her, Janet always said, "My treat" If Louise, too, scored a find.

Louise considered it a positive sign that Janet was interested in buying new clothes for herself, so she kept encouraging Janet to try things on. "You'll need a white button-down with those, and a belt," Louise would say, returning with an armload of garments to throw over the dressing-room door.

Louise had heard Janet tell this story of regret before, or a version of it, anyway. As Janet tried on outfits, Louise would sit on a bench outside her dressing room, listening to Janet.

"I should have spent more time with Mom. Now she's gone, and I miss her. It makes me so glad that we see each other as much as we do, honey," Janet said, emerging from the dressing room in her old clothes. She had worn at least something of her own that day, some old chinos and one of her mother's turtlenecks with beading around the neck. She squeezed Louise with her wiry arms.

Janet fiddled with her earrings before gathering up what she was going to buy. "We should go. I'm sure you have things you need to do," she said.

But Louise didn't. She wanted to tell Janet that she had never been too swamped, never not wanted Janet around, never wished Janet would take her home or hadn't stopped by. She loved being with Janet, and it wasn't just because Janet was generous, buying Louise whatever she needed, from shoes to food to face wash. No, it was something else. Being with Janet was like drinking a potion, a tonic that left her feeling loved, differently than by Nick. It wasn't a better love, simply a different one. Janet's acceptance of Louise was total, even when she was being a huge brat; accepting, for instance, Louise's tendency of complaining of hunger even after just eating, or making Janet stop at gas stations for gum even when they were in a hurry. Or, when visiting Janet for a weekend, her habit of leaving all the lights on downstairs when she went to bed, dropping wet towels on the floor, and generally never lifting a finger. Louise, almost thirty, had never learned to properly clean a bathtub or iron a shirt. But Janet still adored Louise, and Louise could feel it, and never wanted it to disappear.

When Louise became a mother, she often wondered about motherhood. She would think about Janet and the things Janet might feel toward Louise. She understood better now, just as she understood the fear mothers have for their children—fear for their safety, their happiness, their chance for normalcy, fear that some sort of freak accident, some bad luck, might make that chance disappear.

# The Mind 440

Louise was all done with the surgeries to try to make her crook-ed eye straight, done with the operations to make the paralyzed half of her face move. She no longer went to the plastic surgeon to get Botox injections, stopped talking about seeing a specialist in Philadelphia. She had moved on. Almost.

"This is the last thing I need to do before I'm done with doctors completely," she told Nick. "This is the very last thing." She knew one ear worked better than the other. She always tilted her head with her good ear up and forward when speaking to someone so she would be sure to hear them best. It looked like she was posing for a picture. She was getting tired of saying "I know!" (the safest answer) to some words she couldn't understand, of settling back in her chair and letting the others at a restaurant table wind the conversation where they wanted to, of her inability to distinguish all the voices from the background music, the din of dishes, the argument at the next table. There were the mumblers, the quiet talkers, the fast talkers—she never understood much of anything they said. She loved loudmouths. But she wanted to give herself a chance.

During the two surgeries to remove the cavernous angioma, the cranial nerves affecting sensory functions (such as vision and hear-ing) had unavoidably suffered slight damage. The cranial nerves join the brainstem in the pons, the area of the brain where the surgeons had operated. There is no wasted space or room for error in this region of the nervous system.

"If you think you need this, then we'll do it," Nick said. He was used to Louise's sudden obsessions, but this one had come as more of a surprise to him than most. Usually, Louise was convinced she needed something—fish oil supplements, a denim vest, to eat a grapefruit each morning—for a few days, and then the idea would cool and pass. But the idea of a hearing aid, something he thought was only for the elderly or the severely hearing impaired, had stuck with her for weeks. She and Nick were on a walk in their new neighborhood the day before her appointment. They had bought a house in the old part of town, where some people had tidy, ornamented lawns and metal carports, and some houses were soggy, with yards full of rusting car parts.

"I don't think I need it, I know I do," she said, resolutely zipping up her jacket.

Louise always walked too fast for Nick. Sometimes he would ask her to slow down, first joking, then pleading. She would oblige for a while, but she always sped back up.

*

When Louise went in for her appointment with the audiologist, Nick sat outside the padded chamber where she took a hearing test. A large part of the test involved waiting until the first moment she could hear a sound, a knock or a beep, and then raising her index finger to indicate that she had heard it. Louise could see Nick through the window. He looked very serious.

The audiologist wore a white coat, but she had many things about her that were un-doctor-like. She had long hair that she had curled and pulled pieces back with tiny clips. She had charm bracelets and long fuchsia nails, and her ears were pierced all the way up. She had four children, she told Nick and Louise, and had not become an audiologist until they were all out of diapers. This all concerned Louise. She was used to dealing with doctors who were tight-lipped, short-haired, with cufflinks.

After the test, the audiologist said, "Your life is going to be a lot better with a hearing aid," and Louise started to cry. She had never heard a doctor make promise like that. She and the audiologist hugged.

The audiologist recommended a model with optional Zen sound effects when a knob was turned. A fountain trickling or a thunderstorm would be produced. It was called the Mind 440.

"They can be very soothing. One of my daughters has the same one," she said.

She told Louise how to care for it, to swab it with alcohol every night and place it in a portable dehumidifier. The way the tubing was cleaned with a tiny rod looked like threading a needle.

"These things are virtually indestructible. We find my daughter's in her pocket in the laundry hamper, the dog's food bowl, wherever," the audiologist said, flipping her hair.

Louise held it in her hand and she and Nick gazed at it. It was golden and curved, like a seashell. The audiologist put it in Louise's left ear. Her voice sounded electronic to Louise. "That's the way it's supposed to sound," the audiologist said. "You'll get used to it." She ran their credit card through a machine she pulled out of a desk drawer, and Louise signed something. The hearing aid cost as much as a semester of school.

The audiologist stood up. "Bye-bye," she said to Nick and Louise. "Enjoy your new life."

*

As Louise and Nick drove home, she heard creaking in the car that she had never heard before, the swinging of the seatbelts and the rattle of something plastic. In town, passing houses with iron eagles over doors and windows with striped rubber awnings, all of it was beautiful.

She went to a coffee shop to do some grading and could hear people tapping at keyboards and holding whispered conversations with themselves. Outside, she heard birds caw, and the wind created an effect like someone speaking too close to a microphone. At school she kept taking her hearing aid out to wonder at it, and showed it to her friends.

A YouTube video featured a baby with a cochlear implant hearing his mother's voice for the first time as a one-year-old. He grinned and cooed. His life was so much better now. Louise watched it over and over.

After a couple of weeks, Louise noticed that the plastic tube that went into her ear became clogged with wax. Even the cleaning materials, the miniature plastic brush and rod, did no good, the brown goo stayed coated in there, blocking the way for the amplified sound to get through. She discovered she could not wear winter hats, or go on the treadmill at the gym, because tucking her hair behind her ear or pulling fabric over the hearing aid knocked it out of place. She started taking it out when she sat on the couch to read, and forgot to put it back in, only to find the cats batting it around in the middle of the night.

"You wanted this, remember?" Nick said to Louise one cold and dark Saturday afternoon. He had found it in the junk drawer, among the odd sizes of batteries and twisty ties.

"You talked about making the appointment with that audiologist for months. You were so excited. Why don't you get it repaired? Heck, we can send it back and get a new one." He poured himself a mug of that morning's cold coffee, shut the door to the microwave harder than was necessary. He saw Louise's bottom lip begin to wobble.

Louise sat at the kitchen table and was fiddling with the hearing aid again, trying to get it to fit in her ear how she wanted.

"You don't understand," she said, crying. "Instead of making things better this thing just makes things worse."

Nick set his jaw and did not look at her.

"You have to go back to that audiologist and get it fixed. You need to see this through," he said. "You can't just stop doing things all the time." *Get on living*

Other things Louise had started but abandoned:

*The 30-Day Shred*

Drawing comics

Crocheting

*Swann's Way*

a Blackberry

the vegetable garden

raking leaves

Louise abandoned the Mind 440 because it made things worse. It gave piercing feedback, amplified all background noise, and the little plastic tube that went into her ear gave an itch she could never quite scratch. She was always thinking about the Mind 440. Not that she was self-conscious about wearing it—for one thing, she had many other parts of herself to be self-conscious about, and anyway a fair amount of people wore hearing aids. Mostly, she was upset it wasn't better. She wanted the "new life" the audiologist had promised her. She didn't realize until now that she was still looking for a miracle. *Quick fix to life*

\*

Her mother, Janet, took Louise to the audiologist the next time. Nick had to work. When Louise had told Janet she was getting a hearing aid, Janet said, "Your grandfather has one and says they're not all they're cracked up to be," but now here she was.

When Louise's name was called she left Janet sitting in the waiting room. She told the audiologist how her hearing aid was clogged with wax, and the audiologist ushered her into a room with a reclining chair, like a dentist's. Janet heard Louise cry out. She couldn't help rushing past the doors and into the exam room, where Louise was lying in the chair, covering her ear. The audiologist stood there, holding a metal tool, smiling. *Different perspective*

"I know it hurts, but we have to get that sticky wax off of the inner ear," she said. "You'll be fine, it's just a sensitive area. Our mentally impaired patients have an especially hard time with this," she added. *Is Louise mentally impaired?*

\*

Louise had just been called a mentally impaired patient by a doctor with fuchsia nails and piercings up her ear. This was not a high point.

✳

Janet and Louise were silent during the drive home. They didn't speak of the hearing aid after that.

✳

"Maybe you should try a different doctor," Nick said.
"Yes. I should," Louise said. "But an audiologist isn't really a doctor, anyway."

✳

One day, during a slow afternoon in the tutoring center where she worked a few days a week, Louise accidentally snapped a piece of the hearing aid off and it disappeared onto the dirty linoleum. She had been trying to clean it with a bent paper clip.

✳

Louise and Nick went to Minnesota for her brother Michael's college graduation in the spring. The town's main industry was a Malt-O-Meal plant, and the air smelled of cereal. Michael's room-mates and their families had a barbecue after the ceremony, and it poured. Everyone gathered under the park's shelter to eat.

Nick had the hearing aid in his shirt pocket because Louise said it was tickling her ear and couldn't stand it. Even though she had broken off part of the hearing aid, it still worked, for the most part. Later, as she and Nick were driving back to their hotel, Nick couldn't find it in his pocket. He turned the car around.

Louise called Janet, who called Tom, who called Warner, who called Michael. They combed the site of the cookout, but no hearing aid. Michael started to make calls to his roommates. Maybe one of them had seen it?

"Bingo!" he said. "My friend's mom has it! She found it in her cooler, the one that held all the beer. She thought it was her dad's, but now looking she sees it's not. I'll get her address."

"Dude, it must have fallen out of your pocket when you leaned over to get a cold one," Tom said to Nick.

They went to the woman's house. She gave it back in a plastic baggie.

The hearing aid finally stopped working altogether, and Louise didn't know if it was from dirt, the broken piece, or a dead battery.

Nick vowed not to ask Louise about it anymore. He pretended it never happened. But he wondered, doesn't she want it to work? Hadn't it made things better for a while? But the way she looked at him when he told her she needed to get it fixed—she looked scared.

For a while, the hearing aid sat in the portable dehumidifier, the size of a can of nuts, on the bathroom counter. It was there to serve as a visual reminder for Louise to call another audiologist, maybe one in town, so she could drive herself. Maybe she could get a recommendation from somebody, but who did she know who wore a hearing aid?

Then Louise moved the hearing aid to a shelf in the bedroom, where she could still see it. A couple of times she tried it on again, to see if it worked, but nothing. She needed to buy new batteries, but didn't.

*

Then she didn't know where it was. It could be in the middle dresser drawer where they kept things like pregnancy tests and old birthday cards. Or maybe somewhere in her car, in the storage

42

compartment with old parking tickets? Maybe she had brought it out there to make taking it somewhere to get it fixed even easier, the way she kept dirty sweaters in her backseat for the cleaners. Maybe Nick had it. Maybe he was planning to surprise her with a new one, the best on the market. It would be comfortable, fitting in her ear perfectly so that she couldn't even feel it. It would pick up the quiet talkers but turn down the background noise. It would be waterproof, sweat-proof, and she would never hear that splitting feedback whine when too close to a speaker or stereo. It would be like a real ear, but better.

She wants perfection & has unrealistic expectations

# Imagine a Mother

By the third month of trying to get pregnant, Louise had restricted Nick to sex only on the days the calendar deemed super fertile: days 15, 16, and 17 of her menstrual cycle. During those days she contemplated driving to his office in nothing but snow boots and a sundress and pulling down the back seat all the way, but didn't. Sex had to be in the early morning anyway—the time of day was important because a woman's body temperature fluctuated and that affected her eggs, a website said.

Nick began to roll his eyes when she mentioned babies after those first few months of trying. It was all she talked about. Louise had ruined this "trying," and it didn't even take her very long.

She knew she was going about this in the wrong way—getting pregnant was a special time for couples, all the books said. They were supposed to have fun trying, focus on each other and the miracle of life. But her brain had been cut open. When she was in physical rehabilitation afterwards, she learned all sorts of ways to strengthen her body quickly, to get her weakened right side and loss of balance back to the way it used to be. She didn't let nature take its course. Instead, she used rubber resistance bands, small hand weights, and heavy jump ropes every day. Playing jacks increased dexterity, word searches trained the eye. There was nothing better than walking in sand to help balance, and playing the game Connect Four helped with depth-perception. Aqua aerobics, Bikram yoga, acupuncture. Zinc. Hypnosis. Meditation. Low doses of electric shocks. Whatever the doctors suggested, Louise did. She scoured chat rooms and message boards for ideas, too. Bought every tool, took every pill. She exhausted the possibility of failure, until that, too, failed. Sometimes things just didn't work, faces didn't move, eyes didn't follow. That scared Louise. This time was no different. She would try everything until something worked. She realized that a few months was nothing regarding how long it took most couples to conceive—six months to a year was the norm, she had heard—but it didn't matter. Her impatience was rampant. There was no rationalization.

(Almost ) a control freak

They didn't want anyone to know they were trying for a baby. It had to be a secret, Louise and Nick told each other, otherwise the pressure would stress them out. The same week they were supposed to have as much sex as possible they had to be at a family reunion. It was held at the YMCA in the Colorado Rockies, and everyone was staying together in a big lodge, all of them with metal bunk beds and dirty carpeting.

They had a room to themselves, Janet and the Doctor were next door. They left their door open and kept bags of snacks on the bedside table. Cousins were always going in and out with fistfuls of chips and dried fruit. At night, Janet walked around the halls in wet hair and a sleep-shirt talking to everyone. Louise felt bad that this week was the time that she and Nick needed to be alone. Louise was glad to be with Janet; she had missed her. She always did. But she also wanted to become a mother herself, and right now, Janet seemed to be in the way.

On the drive out to Colorado, Louise and Nick stopped at a truck stop and Louise, looking for a bathroom, passed doors with locks that looked like dial pads on pay phones. She could feel heat from steam and smell green, and was very close to a naked stranger, probably a man. Maybe she and Nick should do it in the showers there. That might be the most privacy they would get.

Of course, Louise couldn't decide to have a baby without considering her condition. There was an off-center eye, the immobile half of her face, problems with balance. She had answered questions about her appearance to small children before, explaining that she had a boo-boo, and she wondered how she would explain it to her own child someday. She wondered if it would feel ashamed of her. Or if she would feel ashamed of herself. She remembered how when she was a kid she had noticed that Janet didn't paint her nails or wear makeup like other mothers. One mom in particular used a curling iron every morning and got manicures at a salon with a Greek name. Louise tried to convince Janet to at least wear lipstick. Janet tried, she even got her "colors done" at a department store in Chicago and came home with a bag of products. But they all ended up in a bathroom drawer, mostly unused. Louise had wanted a different mom. How had Janet felt? Louise had never asked. But if she had noticed Janet looking different by being bare-faced, she could bet her daughter might have feelings about her mother with her kind of physical abnormalities. How would Louise deal with that, and with the feeling that there was nothing she could do about it? It might make her daughter a better person, too, Louise acknowledged. More understanding, empathetic to people who dealt with circumstances that were beyond their control. At least there was that.

The big kitchen in the lodge was for everybody, so Louise hid her special fertility tea behind the condiments. She was supposed to drink it in the morning on an empty stomach when she took her prenatal vitamins, which she hid in an outer pocket of her suitcase. They were big yellow capsules that smelled like sardines. Alone in her room, she got online and looked at pregnancy message boards. Posts were titled: WHY CAN'T I GET PREGNANT and WHEN CAN I PEE AFTER SEX? She learned what angel babies were. They were babies that had died.

When she and Nick were supposed to have sex, they told the rest of the family that they were going on a solo hike. Afterwards, Louise got into the candle position for twenty minutes. It was like a headstand, and she had learned that on the Internet, too. When Louise was on her head, she imagined Nick's sperm at the very beginning of their long journey. She was giving them a boost, like riding a bike downhill, she was cheering them on. You can do it. She imagined a Lance Armstrong of sperm pulling away from the peloton and dashing to the finish line.

Louise's cousins and brothers got up at 3 a.m. to climb the tallest mountain in the park, which required ropes and watching for falling rocks. There was a rule that they had to put used toilet paper in their backpacks and hike it down. They didn't want to leave a footprint.

Her father should be the last to know, Louise had heard. She had heard not to tell even her husband right away if she was pregnant. To let that secret be hers for a while. But that was wrong, she thought. She and Nick should share everything as a couple. After all, they will be a family.

One morning, a bunch of people drove to a trailhead where there was a hike to a waterfall. In the backseat, a cousin's boyfriend alternated between talking about how sugar was just as addictive as cocaine and his graduate dissertation on constructing an office building out of plants. His apartment was crammed with them, he said, and so he got more oxygen and felt better than most people.

Louise turned to her cousin. "Do you ever think about having kids?" Louise asked her. She couldn't help it—maybe it was the hormones, stronger during fertile days.

The cousin worked at a running shoe store, made her own almond butter, and ate raw garlic. She looked at Louise like her question was a trick.

"Maybe someday," the cousin said, "but we have so much we want to do. Travel, for instance. At least we got to check India off our list, right honey?"

The cousin looked at her boyfriend, not at Louise.

Louise nodded. She wanted to travel, too, but she and Nick never had the money to go anywhere but St. Louis, where his mother lived. She wondered about taking what she had heard was called a Babymoon, the last vacation a couple took alone before a baby was born. Maybe they would take a Babymoon to St. Louis, or if they waited, maybe they could save up to go somewhere better.

Louise remembered the moment they had said that they wanted to have a baby for sure. They had been in a lake, treading water. She had just lost her sunglasses to the deep water, but had a spare in the car. It had been so easy to make that decision to have a baby, deceptively so. To decide to do it, that is. She hadn't realized at the time that deciding to do something did not equal doing it.

If asked, Louise would have said she wanted to be a mother because—well, she didn't know why, exactly. Maybe it was something about getting a chance. She had once heard someone describe children as "the most interesting people in the world" to their parents. She wanted to know her own.

While some people at the reunion hiked, others went to the Crafts Room to tie-dye T-shirts. Some others went horseback riding where the horses were old and hosts for flies. Some sat in the Commons Room and drank soda. Before dinner, Louise stared at herself in the mirror and tried to imagine herself as a mother. The turned-in eye, half-frozen face. She had never seen a mother like her before.

During happy hour, she watched Nick from across the room, fending for himself with three of her uncles who all stood with their short legs spread far apart, hands in their pockets, comfortable forever.

She sat next to Janet. Janet was wearing one of her sons' college sweatshirts and her face shined with lotion. When she laughed, Louise noticed how much people were liking Janet. Louise reached for Janet and squeezed her hand, then received the squeeze back.

Louise and Nick drove back home at the end of the week and she began buying things. Just a book, at first: *The Conception Chronicles*, a fake-diary of one woman who was TTC (Trying To Conceive). It was terrible but Louise read it twice, even highlighted parts. Her period came. The next month she bought the pregnancy tests, the ovulation kits, the membership to an online calendar that kept track of basal body temperature, for which she needed to buy a special thermometer that she had to stick in her mouth the moment she awoke. She got a special pillow to wedge under her butt to help the sperm travel.

She looked at one website for parents with disabilities, but it seemed to be directed at women in wheelchairs or those who were blind, and she didn't look again. Nothing happened that month. Nothing happened the next month, either.

One night, Nick turned off her favorite show, the *Real Housewives of Beverly Hills*, minutes before it was over. Her favorite character was Kyle, a beautiful mother of five married to an Italian realtor. During a commercial break, Louise had been telling Nick her favorite baby girl names. Her top pick right now was Laurel. "Like the tree," she said.

"Hey!" she said when Nick turned off her show. The bronzed women on the screen were drinking cocktails and yelling insults at each other, their diamond jewelry flashing.

"Weezy," he said, looking at her in such a way that Louise couldn't tell if he was joking or serious. "You've got to chill out with this baby stuff. You are obsessed. You get like this sometimes, I know. But it's stressing me out."

He was serious, Louise decided. He had taken his glasses off and there were red marks on the bridge of his nose. Was he growing a beard?

*

So Louise scaled back. It was Christmas, and she told Nick she didn't care about babies anymore. They went to the grocery store parking lot and bought a real tree. She spent too much money on his present of an electronic map and baked him his favorite, a cream puff. It was made of canned pie dough, cream cheese, powdered pudding mix, and chocolate syrup. When the two of them pulled the wishbone after dinner, she had no idea what he wished for with his victory. She didn't know what to ask for herself.

There were many friends with whom Louise wanted to talk about this whole baby thing, but she chose only one, one who already had a child. Louise broached the subject when they were in her friend's kitchen making a Sesame Street cake for her son's first birthday. Black licorice icing filled the inside of Elmo's mouth.

"Well, we may get pregnant at the same time," the friend said with a wink. "We're going for baby number two."

In college, Louise and this friend went to a party in a barn and the friend leaned back on a standing space heater, smoking a cigarette. After a while she ran her fingers through her hair and removed a fistful. She had burned the back of her bob off. Louise, for her share, wore the wrong coat home and puked all over it.

The friend called a week after her son's birthday party to say she was pregnant.

"Sorry, I'm a Fertile Myrtle," the friend said.

*I wonder why we don't get the friend's name?*

*

When it did happen – just a month later – Louise wanted to call Janet right away, but hesitated. She was sure Janet was in bed, or thought that she might be reading an interesting book or writing in her journal, or having some sort of important conversation with the Doctor, something to do with her recent knee surgery, or his high cholesterol. Janet could be doing any number of things and not want to be disturbed, Louise thought. Janet was like that: you never knew what direction she might go. When Louise was little, Janet took up tennis, and one year for her birthday her first husband, Louise's dad, gave her a nylon warm-up suit of black and pink geometric designs. She started watching tennis on TV while she was ironing, bought a bunch of short, pleated skirts, and joined the city's team. The next year she stopped playing, just like that, and started cleaning the house fervently every night after the kids were in bed, wearing kneepads when she stripped and re-waxed the kitchen linoleum. The next year she started running, and did half-marathons soon after. By the time Louise's parents got divorced Janet had earned her master's in library science by driving into the city three nights a week. She didn't stick with that, though, but did other things, like moving back to Kansas and buying her dad's newspaper.

In high school, friends' parents would always ask, "How's your mom?" with an interested, amused look. Until Louise got sick, that is, and then Janet's life became that. She moved Louise into her house, where the two of them watched movie marathons during the day when Janet should have been working. She helped Louise shower. Read aloud by her bed every night. Louise remembered Janet's wedding reception a few years ago, when she had remarried, finally. She and Louise had held hands at the head table as everyone started to leave for the night. Louise was dating Nick, and life was getting better. Janet looked at her new, sparkling ring and said, "May you be this happy someday."

# Baby Class

The baby class was from 6 to 9 p.m., so lots of couples brought dinner in bags. It met in the hospital's basement, and there were giant rubber balls for the women to sit on, the kind used in gyms, only here they were called "birth balls" and their use was encouraged all the way to the delivery room. Sometimes the class would watch videos on the big projector screen: *Natural Childbirth*, *All About C-sections*, or *How to Swaddle*. The new parents in the films were real, the teacher told them. These were not simulations. The new mothers had large pores and were puffy. The men were in need of haircuts and looked like teenagers. There were a lot of tattoos.

"They must have gotten money to have been taped at a time like that," Nick whispered to Louise. "Talk about desperate."

Louise didn't really care how she had her baby—whether or not to have an epidural, whether her labor would be induced, whether it was her own doctor or one she had never seen before who guided her baby out. She had no interest in hiring a doula or going to the local Birth Center, where only natural childbirth was allowed, and blueberry flax smoothies and comfrey candles were part of the package. She wasn't sure why she cared so little about the actual birth experience—normally she was interested in all things wellness: fish oil supplements, kale, and chia seeds. Now at the end of her pregnancy, she was walking with Nick for thirty minutes at six in the morning before it got hot. She took her special vitamins, attended sessions in prenatal yoga and prenatal aqua aerobics, and downloaded an app that told her what size of fruit or vegetable her baby matched every week. But as to the actual birth itself, Louise wasn't picky. Maybe part of it was that Louise knew by now that in the end she would have little control over what happened. Giving birth, like having brain surgery, seemed terrifying, and there was no sugar-coating that.

*

Some of the women were the kind who seemed uncomfortable in their pregnant bodies, wearing extra-large T-shirts and stiff khakis with stretchy panels over the belly. Other women looked sexy, with capri-length leggings that displayed tanned, shapely calves and tunics that hugged what swelled. Louise was in between—her favorite outfit was a sweater dress that made the bump seem to pop, to be "all belly." Her least favorite item was a pair of too-tight jean shorts.

In a way, she thought that being pregnant might distract from her abnormal appearance. She looked like an average woman involved in something perfectly approved-of by society. Part of her thought her pregnancy might sort of make up for her eye. That part of her body didn't work, but the important parts did, especially the parts that determined and confirmed womanhood. Sure, beauty in its external reality is powerful, but it is external and fleeting. Conceiving and carrying a baby inside your body—that is internal and real. Where one part of her body had let her down, the other had come through in the clutch.

But she also wondered that people might have feelings about whether or not she should be pregnant; or more likely, since most people probably didn't care that much, whether being pregnant simply made her look even weirder and drew even more attention to her. She had gotten over her dislike of wearing jewelry for fear of drawing any attention to herself; she wore earrings now. But still, having people looking at her made her want to disappear.

*

After a few classes, Louise and Nick realized they knew one couple that sat at the table next to theirs, if only vaguely, through friends of friends. The husband was slouched, playing Angry Birds on his phone, and they could hear the sound effects as he shot another bird flying through the sky. His wife looked straight ahead, prettier than Louise remembered, like Snow White.

The teacher began talking about the benefits of breastfeeding, and kept grabbing her own pair to demonstrate positions: the Cradle Hold, or the Football. Louise looked at Nick so he would laugh at this with her, but he was busy scribbling down notes: *Be supportive, even if it means just sitting there*, and *paper towels, bananas.*

During the break Louise and Nick ran into the Angry Birds husband and wife at the vending machines. The women talked about swollen feet (flip-flops, ice baths) and the husbands stood together but separate, the Angry Birds husband still playing the game.

The Angry Birds wife reached across Louise and poked Nick in the bicep. "I'm sorry my husband can't talk to you," she said, her husband acting like he couldn't hear, pressing hard on the keys on his phone. "You see, he's doing something very important. Being a father is stressing him out."

She said the last part in a baby-talk voice.

All week, Louise thought about the Angry Birds couple. What was going to happen once the baby was born? Why did they get married, anyway? Or pregnant? Were those stupid questions? Why did anyone do those things? And, how close were she and Nick to becoming them? Were they a good match? She thought about her friends who were married and had children. They seemed like they were doing O.K. with their partners. But everyone knew so little of how things were between couples, what really went on. Really, no one had a clue. Louise, a child who was relieved when her parents divorced when she was twelve because that meant the tension would go away, had never understood why unhappy couples stayed married "for the kids." But now she was starting to get it. A child was like an agreement between a couple, a project, and once started by both, you wanted to see it through, even if you were miserable. Maybe even especially if you were miserable.

*

After class was over Louise stood by the hospital's front entrance, waiting for Nick to bring the car around. She was past the point of walking much, it wouldn't be long now. She saw the Angry Birds wife waddling toward the parking lot, keys in hand. Her husband drove a motorcycle, she had said.

*

The next class, they got a tour of the labor & delivery wing of the hospital. The teacher pointed out the best features of a birthing room: a wall-mounted television, Jacuzzi tub, and a foldout couch for the fathers. "The cafeteria is on the third floor, it's quite yummy," she said. "Oh, and surround-sound!"

A man in a plain white T-shirt and baggy jeans raised his hand. The woman he was with looked very young, with her hair fixed back tightly enough that it pulled her eyes.

"Can we listen to any music we want?" he said. "What about volume? Can we play it loud?"

Louise and Nick looked at each other and smirked. "Who *are* these people?" she whispered to Nick. "How do they even get through life?"

"I don't know," Nick said. "But it makes me feel better about myself."

Louise wondered if that was part of the appeal of group classes: to compare yourself, see how you stacked up. Was that one of the only self-esteem-builders before jumping off into the unknown? She wondered what the other couples thought of her and Nick. Did they have nicknames for the two of them? Did they talk with each other about the strange tall woman with the crooked eye? She imagined the Angry Birds wife asking the husband if he thought it was possible Louise's baby would be born with a deformed eye. Who knows what questions people asked about her, what stories they invented?

But then again, no one was as obsessed with Louise as Louise. The couples had their own babies to worry about, their own family dramas, their own histories of disease. Who was Louise to think they gave her any thought whatsoever? *Growth!*

Other questions: does the hospital practice hypnobirth? Where do we find castor oil? How much do midwives cost?

When they went back downstairs, everyone got a newborn doll for practice with putting on diapers. The teacher passed around nursing bras so they could all see the different styles and how they worked. One husband put one on over his shirt and laughed. Louise couldn't help but notice that the Angry Birds husband didn't take a doll, nor examine a nursing bra. If he was not playing his game, he was staring at the ground, or his eyes were closed. Louise thought the other women in the class saw the Angry Birds husband too and scooted their chairs away.

After class, Louise and Nick would go out for ice cream, eating it in the car. Usually they had a lot to talk about. But sometimes they were quiet. Louise wondered how different life would be with a baby in the backseat, and she had no idea what Nick was thinking. If she had to guess, maybe he was worried that she would trip while holding the baby, or bump into a doorframe. Maybe he wasn't sure whether she could take care of it, not the way a mother should. She couldn't tell. He did show concern for her hurting herself by, say, tripping and falling over an unseen curb, but he had never said anything about fearing for the baby's safety while in her care. But he had to have thought it, right? At her worst moments she herself thought about it, so why not Nick?

Or maybe, just like everybody else in their baby class, he was most worried about himself, and how he might get in his own way.

# Birth Plan

More than anything, Louise was worried about her right leg during labor. The reflex was ultra-sensitive since the surgeries had caused some nerve damage, and during all of her examinations during her pregnancy the leg had a mind of its own, sometimes springing out of the stirrup and kicking the doctor lightly. The rest of the birth process seemed darkly unpleasant, but scary? No.

*Do we know Janet's husband's name?*

Janet and the Doctor waited with Nick's mother, Veronica, in the waiting room.

"I can't believe I'm going to be a grandmother!" Janet kept saying. "Oh, yes I can, yes I can. What should I be called? Grammy? Nana? How about Mimi?"

Janet had bought a present for the baby, whom Louise and Nick had said they were going to name Olive: a little pink hair bow. She clutched it in her lap.

*Foreshadowing? No baby?*

\*

Her leg might have kicked, but no one, not even Louise, noticed. There were too many other things going on: contractions, pushing, counting, breathing. When she gave the last push she felt like her stomach went out between her legs, and she couldn't believe she had done it. Nick cut the cord, and when a nurse put Olive in

Louise's arms Nick had the presence of mind to snap a photo. Just like any other mom and dad, Nick and Louise gazed at their new baby, Louise whispering "She's perfect," over and over again. When family was allowed to burst through the door Olive was clean and swaddled, and looked at everyone with wide gray eyes. Louise didn't think to check and see whether or not they were "normal." For that moment, for that day, all those worries left her.

So what's going to change?

# What She Saw

As Olive's eyes grew capable of staying open for more than a few seconds at a time, after a week or so, Louise was finding it unnerving. Her baby kept looking at her, just gazing. Olive's eyes were long-lashed and she rarely blinked, and everyone said they would stay sky blue like Louise's. Olive saw Louise's naked face, the large pores on her cheeks, the blackheads on her small, upturned nose, and her chapped, red lips. They saw the way the moving side of Louise's mouth pulled over the paralyzed side when Louise spoke, saying "Olive, are you hungry?" and the way her adept left fingers helped her stiff, weak right ones with her nursing bra. They saw Louise's smudged glasses with the dark-green frames. It made Louise uncomfortable, that stare, but she was also impressed by its intensity. This baby was going to watch all she pleased. Louise did not like being looked at, but she was beginning to see she would have to get used to it.

Baby looks at her w/ love

# The Root

Before Olive was born, Louise tore up the neighbor's fence with her Subaru. After that, she developed a fear that her foot would not find the brake on her car. It was more than a fear—it consumed her. She had gone through the chain-link because she had pressed the gas instead of the brake while trying to veer around Nick's car. It had been early in the morning, 6:30 or so. Scarf weather, a navy sky. Her peanut butter toast breakfast sat on a napkin in the passenger's seat, NPR was on, and all of a sudden there she was, her headlights reflecting way too close to the neighbor's house.

She had read about old women doing this sort of thing.

The fence was ruined, and she had even put a divot into the house, hit it hard enough that the neighbor, Vicki, later said she felt the house shake. Louise had had to knock on her own front door because she had locked it when she left, and had to do it pretty loud because Nick was asleep with the white-noise machine on. He had come to the door, worried and in his boxers, and she had to spill the story to him right there, while the car, still on, was caught up in the metal fence just out of view.

"It's these damn shoes," she had said.

They were flats.

Ever since then, every time she was at a stoplight, she thought she could feel her right foot slowly slipping off the brake pedal, and she would clamp her foot down, leg aching, until the light turned green. She imagined her foot missing the brake, the car careening off a bridge, into a store window, a passer-by. The screaming. She contemplated getting a car that had a hand brake, like one that a paraplegic would drive.

She searched "fear of driving" on the Internet. Came up with $137 Home-Study programs and downloadable hypnosis recordings. Bought a five-dollar meditation podcast and listened to it once.

She looked to see that her foot was really on the pedal, had to see it with her own eyes, before starting the car, every time.

Her therapist said it went back to a fear of losing control over her life. Again. *Desire for control is very strong*

"That's the root of this whole problem," the therapist said. "It's purely psychological. Now get out and enjoy your day!"

Louise tried.

*

Louise had passed a special driving test, in Michigan, where she had lived with her father and stepmother for several months after her brain surgeries. Officially, it was a driving rehabilitation program through a hospital, but it seemed just like the test Louise had taken as a teen. The point was to test whether Louise was competent to drive with her new, altered vision. When she drove, Louise put Scotch or masking tape over the left lens of her glasses so she would not see double. This helped. None of her doctors had any comment about this arrangement. "Sometimes I think I should do something better than tape over them," Louise would say to Nick. "When the tape comes off, there's this gunk on my glasses that's hard to clean." There were also two-inch strips of tape all over her dashboard and passenger's seat. But neither she nor Nick came up with a solution. So Scotch tape it was.

\*

Louise wore shoes only with thin soles so that she could feel whether her foot was resting lightly on top of the pedal—blue Keds with the laces taken out. Made sure never to come close to tailing another car so there would be no sudden stops. Plenty of time. She had certain routes around town, streets with the least traffic, and she never drove during rush hour. But there were always a few seconds when she would be going down, say, Elm Street, past Woodlawn Elementary, a two-story brick building that little kids would flee at three in the afternoon, and a darting little boy in a red coat would cause her to slam her foot down in a panic.

\*

For a while Louise stopped driving completely. It just seemed easier. If Nick were going out of town to shoot a basketball game, he would drive her to the grocery store before he left. She'd stock up on cans of soup, frozen burritos. She tried taking the city bus up to campus to teach or take classes, but a ten-minute trip by car took an hour or longer on the bus. She got some awkward rides home from classmates. Conversations with people who gave one-word answers. The main thing was she felt like such a loser. "Loser. Loser." That would replay in her head as she walked through her day. She felt like she couldn't do anything. Everyone could drive, it couldn't be that hard. What was wrong with her?

\*

In a way, this not-driving was lonelier than the brain surgeries, because the cavernous angioma was a serious condition that had to be fixed by surgeons. It warranted surgeries, two, in fact, and her

64

medical insurance paid for it. Real doctors at one of the best medical clinics in the world spoke to her and her family in kind tones.

She told few people about it. What she said usually went something like, "I don't like to drive, it kind of freaks me out."

She was especially embarrassed about wearing the tape on her glasses. On the rare occasion that she gave someone else a ride (Nick always drove when they were together) she always went into a long justification of the square of tape.

"Oh well. Whatever it takes to keep us safe," the friend would say with a nervous laugh.

*

Accidents:

Rear ended a lawn-care truck. Car: Oldsmobile Alero, 2001. Red. Four door. Damage: Small dent in front bumper.

Hit by another car at a two-way stop the other driver thought was a four-way. Louise was following Nick to the mechanic's to get new tires. Car: 1998 Volvo Cross Country. Dark Green. Four door. Total loss.

Minor parking lot scrape. Social Security Office parking lot, where Louise was getting Stauffer changed to Krug. No damage to speak of. Car: Subaru Impreza, 2002. Silver. Four Door.

Single-car incident at gas station. Olive was in the car, and Louise was getting gas. When she drove away she heard a crunch and thought she had forgotten to take the pump out. Instead, she had turned too tightly and was scraping the metal pole protecting the pump. Car: Subaru Impreza, 2002. Silver. Four door. Slight dent with a red tinge.

The windshield of the Subaru needed to be replaced from a pheasant smacking into it at 73 mph on Highway 80, near Colby, Kansas.

*

It wasn't right after the surgeries that her driving-phobia started. At first, Louise drove everywhere, at all hours of the day or night, in any weather. On the highway even. Well, once. That had been too scary to ever do again. She would drive to the other side of town at 9 p.m. to the good grocery store, the car lights in the opposite lane shining into her eye that couldn't squint, her nystagmus making the lights bounce and blur together, dancing in jagged patterns. She didn't care. Louise was still smoking then, and sometimes would miss the cracked window to flick her ash through and singed the car's ceiling instead.

Maybe it had something to do with meeting Nick, who always suggested that he drive, at first, and after a while it just became assumed—an unspoken agreement between them that he could do it better. It probably also had to do with the accident Louise had in her Volvo, the one where she was following Nick. The car had been pretty banged up, even though Louise was fine. However it happened, that confidence she had shortly after her surgeries had faded, and now she just felt vulnerable, unfixable, and beat.

*

When Olive came, Louise's driving got better instead of worse. She and Olive went to the library, the pool, grocery shopping—anywhere in town. It was like she had gotten over it. Sometimes Louise would say to Nick, as they were putting their laundry away, "Remember when I didn't drive?" like it was so long ago. They referred to that time as the "dark days" with a laugh. But then, slow-ly, she started getting scared again, tapping the brake pedal every few seconds just to see if it was still there, forgetting to breathe, imaging her and Olive crashing into the car in front of them, air-bags blowing up, glass breaking, someone calling Nick. After a few days of this she would be O.K. driving without a thought, and then a month later the fear would return again. This cycle continued over and over. She doubted it would ever go away.

*

Maybe they should move to a city; that would solve this whole thing, Louise had thought. She could take the subway or train to work, and Olive would learn to do it, too. But Louise didn't really want to live in a city, or more accurately, hadn't ever imagined it. She had always thought she would have a house with a yard, and Olive would live in a neighborhood with lots of other kids in it, and play with them in the street after dinner. Louise had thought she would be the one to drive Olive around—to music lessons, friends' houses, the grocery store. She had thought they would live that kind of life. But then, Louise had thought a lot of things. Thinking things didn't mean jack.

# Therapist

Louise went to see her therapist after a long hiatus. The last time she had been in her office had been before she was pregnant. Louise couldn't remember exactly why she had stopped seeing her, but now she wanted to give the therapist an update. Things were hard between her and Nick sometimes. Olive was still a baby, and Louise and Nick got a scant amount of sleep. Each thought that they did more chores than the other—they kept score. Louise felt like she weighed a million pounds. There were worries about money and sex, or the lack of both. Louise thought maybe her therapist could help her out, even if they hadn't had much success in the past.

"I can tell you're breastfeeding!" the therapist said when Louise sat down on the couch.

"And I like your new glasses," the therapist added.

The therapist was a very handsome woman, one whom Louise wanted to look like one day. Her gray hair was short, worn in a cap style, and she usually had interesting earrings and scarves. She occupied her chair in a way that looked graceful, with her neck stretched and hands moving.

"So, I found this recipe for a farro and tomato salad that you have got to try," the therapist said, and Louise remembered this was one reason she had stopped seeing her—they ended up talking about cooking and yoga (they had the same teacher for a while) instead of doing what they were supposed to, and Louise hadn't felt very good about that. This time, like all the other times, she said, "Tell me!" and took out her phone to take notes. She couldn't help herself. Maybe she was lonely.

The therapist also talked about her daughter a lot, and after she finished telling Louise about the farro and tomato salad, she began filling Louise in on her daughter's living situation in London. Apparently, she had a very important job in science and a baby, and her husband was a lout.

Louise remembered the first recipe the therapist gave her, that dark winter she had first moved back. Her days were lonely, and she did things like put her clothes in trash bags and haul them to a laundromat across town. It really wasn't a recipe at all that the therapist had told her, more like a tip. There was a dehydrated lentil soup mix that was available at the health food store. The therapist told her to add boiling water to some of the soup mix and have a hunk of brown bread with it. An easy meal, she had called it. But nourishing. The first winter Louise was her patient she had eaten that many times.

"So, what brings you here?" the therapist said. "Why today? Why did you come in?"

"Well, you know, it's hard at home, sometimes. Being married and everything. Babies make things hard . . ." and Louise trailed off. This was the trouble with her and therapy—she could never bring herself to be honest, to tell the therapist anything specific for fear of sounding ridiculous, such as: if my parents got divorced, and my grandparents did too, does that mean I will?

The therapist just looked at her and smiled, and that was all it took for Louise to start to cry. "Of course it's hard. It's O.K.," the therapist said. "You just need to take it one day at a time."

Louise nodded. She remembered now why she had really stopped seeing the therapist. Her last session had been awkward. Louise was trying to tell the therapist a story about Janet, or rather, a story Janet had told her recently that had made her sad.

"My mom said that one Halloween, when my brother Michael was still pretty little, she was so depressed she couldn't get up the energy to make sure we had costumes," Louise had said. "Isn't that horrible? That just makes me want to cry."

"I'm sorry, I don't understand," the therapist had said. "Why? Why does that seem so sad to you?"

"I don't know, it just does," Louise said. "It is sad. It's a sad thing to be depressed, and little kids don't know that their mom feels that way. I don't remember that time. I wish I did. Then I could have helped her."

"But it wasn't about you," the therapist said. "It was just something she was going through. Not everything has to do with you, you know."

Louise had bristled. Didn't her memories have to do with her? If an event affected her, didn't that count? But she couldn't share any of this with the therapist. It was so hard, impossible, to sit there and tell someone exactly what you were thinking. She was a Midwesterner about social interactions—they should be comfortable, pleasant, and gratifying. Even with therapists. It was so much easier to tell the whole truth in writing. That was probably the biggest reason she had written her first book, her memoir about her brain surgeries. Writing it down and putting it in a document to digest and understand was so much easier than discussing a situation.

Which was another thing. Her therapist would often say, "But look at all you've accomplished. You wrote a book!" This pained

Louise, because writing a book had nothing to do with some aspects of her life. Lots and lots of people wrote books. There were probably too many books out there, she would be willing to argue. She was glad she had written one and grateful for its publication. That she still couldn't fit into any of her pre-baby clothes and cried in the examination room at the doctor's office when she was told her weight, that had nothing to do with whether or not she'd written a book. She felt like she couldn't, or shouldn't have to, explain this to the therapist. And what if the therapist was right? Should Louise just count her blessings and get on with it? Was she expecting too much?

After the post-baby visit to the therapist, Louise stopped going to therapy for good. "Maybe I'm just not good at therapy, kind of like hypnosis or meditation," she thought. "I just can't let go and let the therapist help me—I care what she thinks, I can't help it." It was crazy to want to pretend that you were O.K. to the professional you paid to help you, but that was what she had done. She wondered whether the therapist could tell that she was putting a veneer on her feelings, if she could sense it, smell it like a drug dog. Probably. It wasn't that hard to tell when other people were lying, and if you told that lie enough you started to believe it, too.

# No Noises

Louise had to get a child a birthday present, and it couldn't be noisy. It had to do with something the parents believed in. No batteries, either. Wooden toys were popular, Louise noticed. She saw them in the small, costly children's shops downtown. Child-sized maracas with the label "1+" so the buyer would know the toy was for one-year olds and older. Wooden fake-food, such as bacon or a mound of mashed potatoes for a play-kitchen that a father would build out of logs.

She was not sure whether the preference for no noisy toys was for reasons aesthetic, environmental, or health—was it that battery operated toys prohibited learning? Or stunted creativity? There was something about plastic, also. She vaguely remembered something about certain kinds of chemicals found in plastic that could be released if children were to chew on them. Or, there were two kinds of plastic toys, right? The good and not-good kind. That sounded correct. It was easy to tell between the two because there were so many labels on everything, letting you know you were doing the right thing.

Since Louise had had a baby she had met lots of conscientious mothers. These mothers did not want their babies to swim in pools cleaned with chlorine, or to wear disposable diapers, or to be vaccinated. They did not want fluoride in the city water. They wanted to take their children on field trips to farms that let the children drink raw milk that had not been pasteurized. They switched to Traditional Eating, which touted gravy, kombucha, and meat.

Louise could not keep straight why each thing was wrong, which chemicals were in fluoridated water and which were in vaccines, which problems were associated with chlorine. A popular discussion topic for the mothers of the town was Baby-Led Weaning, which involved letting one's baby feed herself from the very start—for example, letting her gum an apple core or suck on a hunk of red bell pepper instead of spooning pureed peas into her mouth. Baby-Led Weaning was said to prevent obesity later in life, but one had to watch the babies at all times to prevent choking.

The most desirable school was on the edge of town, where the children all wore identical gray smocks and carried the same metal lunch pail. The teachers called them "friends" and the children did things like make soap. This was a very expensive school that Louise could not afford.

*

Louise told Nick about the no-noise birthday present as they ate dinner that night. They were eating toad-in-a-hole. Louise looked at Olive, who watched an educational children's show from the floor of the living room, grinning at the puppet on the screen, a dog with his tongue sticking out of the side of his mouth.

"What do people think these toys could realistically do in a lifetime?" Nick said. He cut the yolk with the side of his fork and swirled a piece of toast in it.

"I don't know," Louise said. "Maybe they are doing the right thing, though. Maybe we should read more, be more educated about Olive's well-being."

Nick checked his email but kept eating. "You don't always have to do what everyone else is doing, Louise. I think we do a pretty good job."

"I know that," she said, taking a big bite, yolk running down her chin. But at the same time, she didn't know that. It was always better to be more cautious than less, right? Always better to be safe? She looked at her daughter, so happy, but this T.V. show was almost surely bad for her in some way. Their doctor had said Olive was supposed to sit in her high chair at the table with them so they could show her that families ate dinner together, but Olive screamed and squirmed until they let her free.

*

The next morning, Louise and Olive went to the public swimming pool. One of the mothers who was against noisy toys was there, wearing a no-nonsense black tank-style swimsuit. Louise and Olive joined the other mothers in the water who were pulling their babies around, making noises like motorboats. After a while they sat on the grass and fed their babies pieces of strawberries and banana. They talked about real estate. Everyone wanted a bigger house. The no-noisy mother said, "I just want someplace where I have enough land to have a real garden, to get out and hoe a row before breakfast." She had eaten pieces of her placenta on hummus with pita chips the day after she gave birth in her bathtub. She said it was a miracle food.

Louise hadn't done anything like that. She had given birth to Olive in the hospital and had had an epidural. Two, actually, because the first one had worn off (even though the nurses had said that couldn't happen, that it was all in her head). She remembered being numb below the waist and eating Jell-O and popsicles and laughing at some movie while her contractions spiked. Maybe she should have been doing something else instead.

The no-noisy toys mother got up to leave, slipping her baby into a pouch on her hip. She made it look so easy.

"Nice toy," she said, looking at Louise and then at the toy in Olive's hands, a set of plastic wind-up chattering teeth. Louise had found them at a joke shop.

＊

Or at least, saying so would have made it better, Louise told Janet. "Really, all that happened was that she smiled at me before she walked home from the pool. She and her husband share one car. You know, to conserve."

Janet babysat Olive on Thursdays while Louise taught, and now they were in Louise's kitchen, making dinner. Or rather, putting grocery-store sushi on plates while Olive sat in her highchair, picking at macaroni.

"You mean because if the mother was mean you could have disliked her?" Janet said.

"Right," Louise said. "As it was, she seemed like a good mom and a kind person. Or fine, at least. As nice as me, for sure."

That was true, Louise realized. She was not nicer than anyone else she knew when it came to parenting. She often wondered whether the mothers whom she criticized for not vaccinating their children for fear of side effects or sleeping in a "family bed" ever made fun of mothers like her for using strollers and toys that made noise. She almost hoped they did. That would make things more even, if everyone talked shit about everyone else, if the parents who home-schooled were as judgmental as those who paid their kids for good grades. Then maybe differences would be meaningless, the mothers whose kids lived at daycare the same as the mothers who stayed home and had the wherewithal to come up with new arts and crafts projects every day, using scary things like glitter and scissors. They would all be horrible people and unworthy of having children. None of them would be doing the right thing, and they would all be executing their worst fear: messing up their kids with no one to blame but themselves. That would be something they could all agree on. And probably more true.

# ESFJ

Sometimes Louise worried that she and Nick fought too much. She remembered how Janet would go out for a walk after an argument with Louise's dad and sometimes be gone for a while. Louise had never done that. She had cried in the bathroom, or at the kitchen table, or their bed, and she had gotten in her car, even started it, but she had never driven away.

*

Louise was happy she was an ESFJ: Extroverted, Sensing, Feeling, Judging. She had taken the Myers-Briggs personality test on her computer. The ESFJ's profile was titled The Caregiver. Nick found out he was an ISFJ when she made him take the test after breakfast one day, standing up at the kitchen counter because that was the only place he could use his computer while it charged. The I in his ISFJ stood for Introverted, and his title was The Nurturer.

"This is exactly right on," Louise hooted, reading the description over his shoulder. One sentence read, "ISFJs have a very clear idea of the way things should be, which they strive to attain."

"Like when you thought my idea of hanging stained glass with fishing line in the kitchen window looked country," she said. "And how you like bacon but won't eat ham."

"Well, that's how I feel," Nick said, pouring more coffee and putting his mug in the microwave. "What's the difference between a caregiver and a nurturer, anyway?"

*

Louise remembered getting ESFP, The Entertainer, as her result a long time ago. She had changed since after the surgeries, she guessed, become more reserved, perhaps, or maybe her evolution was simply part of growing older. But still—an entertainer was nothing like a caregiver. What had happened? What had been the cause of this shift? She speculated it had something to do with becoming a mother—who was more of a caregiver than a parent?

Louise also liked to read about the compatibility of her and Nick's astrological signs. She was a Gemini and he was a Sagittarius, and Louise thought they both fit their signs pretty well. One website said the two signs would attend lots of wild parties together and make each other shine brighter. Gemini, Louise's sign, were natural intellectuals, charmers, gifted with talk. A few other sites said that Gemini were generally two-faced and selfish, indecisive and flighty. Sagittarius, Nick's sign, were Steady Eddies. They were truth-seekers and wanted to know things like the meaning of life. Their worst trait was tactlessness. Louise felt like these descriptions were accurate for herself, but not for Nick. He always said he liked even her worst clothing choices or haircuts, and tended to diffuse misunderstandings between him and everyone else. As for him being a truth-seeker, it was hard to say. What did that really entail? He didn't go to church but said he believed in God. He was more interested in the world around him than she—she was always the last to know about current events, checking her email much more often than reading any news. But as far as knowing why he was alive and what it meant, Louise guessed that neither of them wanted to know that much. Who could say? She had never met anybody who could, really, or who at least would admit that they had even wondered such a thing. Not when there were so many other things to worry about, such as what to make for dinner and how to make time for sex. Those things seemed much more important, much more needing of her attention, than knowing what she was doing on this planet. That was anyone's guess.

*

Louise stopped reading her teaching evaluations from students for a while, after seven students used the adjectives "scatterbrained" and "flighty" to describe her. She thought this could be because she sometimes would go on tangents when talking to students, and didn't always know their names. But she never forgot papers or failed to update the online grade book. Maybe it was because of her blond hair. Or because she laughed at things that weren't funny. Or did it have something to do with how she looked, her trouble holding eye contact or hearing soft-spoken students?

Louise was often curious about how her students saw her, literally, at the front of the classroom. She got to look at twenty different faces, but for them there is only hers to look at. And since she was the one disseminating wisdom, data, details, they had to look at her. They had to focus on her, on the part of her body that people focus on when listening. She wondered how often they would talk about her and it outside of class. Did she have a nickname? Professor Lazy Eye? Professor Crooked? Do they expect more from her because of this? Would they give normal-looking professors more leeway in class evaluations?

*

Louise and Nick were both oldest children. That did not bode well for their union, said a birth-order book Louise had checked out from the library. They had problems sharing things, from a bowl of ice cream to the bathroom sink during teeth brushing. They had Last Word Syndrome, and would endure the silent treatment for only a few minutes before picking the scab of an argument.

*

Their last serious fight had been about Louise buying things that Nick deemed unnecessary. During a three-day period when Nick had been in Texas photographing basketball games, Louise had bought the following items online: a four-pack of toothbrushes called Surround (because they cleaned three surfaces of the teeth at once) for Olive; a sea-salt grinder; a pair of khaki shorts for herself; a portion-control plate called Meal Measure, which had three circles for protein, vegetables, and starch; and a one-ounce bottle of Moroccan Oil for her hair.

Louise's defense was that she was lonely when Nick was gone. She woke up early no matter what, too.

"It's 6 a.m., Olive's sleeping, and I'm sitting around with my computer," she said, smiling, hoping Nick would meet her eyes. But Nick was pretty pissed. Olive was eating a snack in her high chair, toast and hummus, which Nick had cut for her in small, precise squares.

"I'll go to the post office right now and send the plate back," Louise said. "Okay.?"

After ten minutes she came back to the kitchen empty handed. "I can't find it," she said. "I know I put it in there. It's just such a

80

mess in that room, all those clothes and shoes." There was a silence, and then Nick said what he had to say. He had said it many times.

"It's O.K., Louise. It didn't cost that much anyway. Have some toast."

He was a Nurturer.

# Colorado

Every summer since her brain surgeries, Louise wished she hadn't gone to Colorado. But every summer, she went. This would be the sixth summer. Being around all those family members who oozed health, their talk about miles hiked, cliffs climbed, blisters, belay ropes, sore shins—all with grins—it made her sad. She didn't feel sorry for herself. She was used to her body and its limitations. But when she went to Colorado, she got angry again, and she felt sheepish when her heart got dark, but it did. It made her think, "Silly me, I actually thought I was over this."

*

This cabin wasn't just somewhere in Colorado, it was in Rocky Mountain National Park, entered through the town of Estes Park. The mountains were unavoidable. The town was a prepackaged family vacation, chock-full of fudge and ice-cream shops, mini golf, and old-time photo studios. It had stores that sold only rocks, or T-shirts, or saltwater taffy, or Christmas ornaments. Tourists could pay to ride an ancient, exhausted horse on a dusty trail or drive up high on Trail Ridge Road to see snow and little blue flowers. As a kid, Louise's favorite place had been the Lazy B Ranch, a place that served everyone the same tin plate of beans, corn bread and gray beef on a long bench while a group sang onstage.

Every summer various branches of Janet's family gathered in Colorado. Louise's uncles were muscle-bound and liked talking about their younger years of working on Trail Crew: scrambling up mountains to rescue people, carving footpaths out of mountainsides, lifting boulders. Her aunts, who talked a good game about disliking hiking and wanting nothing more than a pedicure and a good movie, were just as bad, tagging behind their husbands on almost every hike.

Her cousins, young, beautiful women with muscle-y stomachs and long-haired boyfriends, they all stayed up late by the fire, slept for three hours and were gone up a peak before breakfast every day.

\*

But Louise had once been like that, sort of. She had grown up doing this. She had done Mount McHenry's when still a teen, starting up the trail at 3 a.m. and not getting back until dinner. She had walked switchbacks until her legs throbbed, sang Peter Paul & Mary while carefully positioning her feet on scree, ate PB&J while in a boulder field, waiting out a hailstorm. She had always complained more than other people, though, and identified more with her father, Warner, who had a quieter love of the outdoors (think bird-watching and bee-keeping, walks). Louise liked to read and eat cookies, but she could hike if she had to, which on family vacations, she had to. Maybe that was another angle to the depression that set in while in Colorado. When she went there, she was reminded of who she used to be and what she used to be able to do, and she wasn't ready to accept that she'd changed. She also was not ready to accept the fact that identity and self-perception are fluid and are dramatically influenced not only by the present but also the past, especially as they relate to each other. Louise knew that her notion of self would have been different if she had *always* had the crooked eye and bad balance. It's the shift, the change, the evolution and devolution out of one's control that shapes one's ability to cope.

But maybe she hadn't really changed that much. Maybe, deep down, whenever she was in Colorado she had always felt that when she was there, she wanted her to be someone she wasn't. She loved parts of Colorado. Making the rounds of visiting their favorite downtown spots: Bob & Tony's Pizza, the bookstore with the great poster collection, the whiffs of the fudge shops, Indian Village and all its plastic souvenirs. Driving up Trail Ridge road and testing her fear of heights as they all stood at the lookout points and saw the whole world before them. After dinner at the cabin, the fireplace, the reading, the s'mores. But does love cancel what you hate? Does it work like that? Louise didn't know.

*

This time, Olive was almost one year old, so this would be her first time at the cabin. At first, as Louise, Nick, and Olive drove out from Kansas, Louise was excited. She had packed pretzels and grapes in snack bags, bought cooking magazines, Olive had Elmo and Nick had the radio: they were on vacation. There was that thrill of staring at flat yellow fields for six hours and then seeing the outline of a purple mountain range, of rolling down the windows after Boulder to suck in the sweet, green air, of passing avalanche signs, stocked trout streams, and suddenly, finally, of dipping down into the valley of Estes Park, the car seemingly pushed into the arms of the town.

Louise began to feel just a prick of regret as she got out of the car, across the uneven ground up to the cabin into the arms of cousins, aunts, uncles, her own brothers, and Janet. She took in the log cabin, the kitchen with its ugly, brick-like linoleum and antique iron stove, at the long dinner table with the blue-and-white checked oil-cloth. The front porch with its million-dollar view. She loved it all. But then, later, after she'd put Olive to bed and sat in the dark on the porch with everybody, someone asked about tomorrow. What should the hike be tomorrow? Chapin? Chiquita? What about Flattop? Who wants to run the whole way?

"Let's do something that Louise can do," Janet said. "What about Emerald Lake? Or Cub? We'll all go," she said. "It's about being together."

"Yeah, great idea," Nick said, and Louise's brothers and cousins echoed him.

"What do you feel like doing, Weezy? Let's do whatever you want," a cousin said.

They decided on Emerald Lake, an easy two miles on a clear path, and everyone moved on to talking about the tree disease that was killing all the pines in the park. Louise had trouble following. She was thinking that now tomorrow was taken care of, what about the next day, and the day after that? She couldn't relax.

Louise was hopeful as they started up the trail the next morning, Olive in a pack on Nick's back. She had two walking sticks, the lightweight aluminum kind, one in each hand. The trail was cement, like a sidewalk. They walked for a while, then reached the lake. They ate some turkey sandwiches while standing up. Drank water even though they weren't thirsty. They hiked back down to the car in twenty minutes.

It was only mid-morning as they pulled up to the cabin, and the rest of her family kept seated as Louise, Nick, and Olive got out.

"You guys go on in and relax," an uncle said. "We're going to do another hike since it's so early in the day and all. Nothing big.

See you for dinner!" And the van rattled down the long gravel driveway again, leaving a cloud.

Well, what did she want? Louise asked herself, sitting on the steps while Nick put Olive down for a nap inside. Easy hikes were short, there was no way around it, and doing too much was disastrous, as she had learned.

Take last year, for example. Someone had suggested doing Ouzel Falls, which was a short, shady hike, but everyone had forgotten how rocky the trail was. At first, it was fine. Louise and Janet held hands and talked. After a quarter mile or so, the trail sloped dramatically and got jagged, and Louise started to slip each step she took. "These damn things," she said, and threw the walking sticks in the woods, with Janet running to retrieve them. By the time they had been hiking for almost an hour, Louise had one arm linked through Nick's and one through Janet's, with them pulling Louise up the trail as her feet dragged behind. The river rushed parallel to their path, and the woods were dark and soft with trees. Louise was crying.

Louise almost didn't go back to Colorado after that summer. "Why?" she would say to Nick, when they would discuss it. It would be late, Olive asleep for hours, and they would be sitting on the couch with their respective computers, trawling their nightly websites. "Why put myself through that kind of frustration when I don't have to? It's a vacation, for Pete's sake. Let's go visit my dad, or your mom, or go somewhere we've never been before. We don't need Colorado." She shut her computer, then opened it. She didn't know what to do.

Nick took off his glasses and rubbed his face. "We don't have to go there. But it's there, Louise. Colorado will always be there, and you can't just ignore it. Your family's there. And it's gorgeous.

We just have to make it work. It will, but it may take a while to feel normal."

She knew he was right, but she didn't know whether it was possible. How could sitting out feel normal?

*

They went out to Colorado again the next summer, when Olive was almost two years old. Nick, Louise, and Olive did a few short hikes, with days in between spent walking through the grassy meadows and going into town buying Olive trinkets such as plastic ponies and little tom-tom drums. It was a bit easier this time, being different from the rest of the clan, getting back to the cabin hours before the serious hikers did, and the lack of an "adventure of the day" story to tell at dinner (Janet saw a moose one day, a cousin almost got blown off a rock face the next). But for the most part, Louise felt content. The air smelled like sage, and one of her aunts made amazing dirty martinis. Near the end of their week, Louise, Nick, and Olive went on a hike to Dream Lake, one mile up. They walked up pretty easily, and were walking around looking for a spot to each lunch when Louise slipped on some gravel, caught one foot on a tree root, and fell down hard. She was wearing shorts, the ground was all rocks, and the scrape on the back of her left thigh was bad. A stranger patched Louise up as best she could (Louise and Nick had no first aid), but when they started to head down, Louise took a few steps and started crying.

"Never again," she said to Nick. "I don't want to hike ever again."

Olive was screaming in Nick's backpack. Bloody bandages were hanging off Louise's leg. Two more strangers stopped Louise at various points on the trail and offered fresh gauze, painkillers, and ointments. They made it back to the car.

They didn't hike the next day, but on their last day there, they did. A small one, so short that Louise said, "This is it?" when she saw the waterfalls. She felt a little mad, a little bored. "Now what?" she asked Nick. "It's only nine in the morning."

"I know," he said. "We have the whole day left."

"What we remember, and how we order and interpret what we believe to be true, are what shapes who we are."

—**Stephen Elliott**, *The Adderall Diaries*

# Short Hair

Louise couldn't decide whether or not to get short hair. The cut she was thinking about was called a "pixie," and when she looked at photos of celebrities with such a style, they looked as though they had just woken up, run their fingers through their gamine cut, and thrown on a gown. On one hand, short hair would feel good in the summertime, Louise thought, her neck able to breathe, no more searching for a ponytail holder or feeling thousands of strands stuck to her skin. She had gone with Janet last week to get Janet's cut. Janet had dark, wavy hair that had been long since Louise was a teenager. Janet wanted it short so she could swim during her lunch hour, and she also wanted to grow out her gray hair, to stop coloring it every month. She read blogs like *Rock the Silver* to prepare for the chop.

At the salon, the hairstylist gathered Janet's thick ponytail in one hand and cut with the scissors, just as Louise had expected she would. Janet looked at Louise with her teeth clenched and her hands between her knees.

"It's so liberating!" Janet said over the phone a week after the cut. "I just get out of the shower, run some goop through it, and I'm done!"

Louise was jealous.

On the other hand, though, Louise thought about her face. "How do you know if short hair is for you?" a website said. "Do you have a perfectly symmetrical face? If not, short hair can bring out your flaws. Remember, there's nowhere to hide with short hair!" The site also said, "A pixie cut is not for those who have extra weight. Who wants a big bottom and a small top? You don't want to look like a pinhead!" Louise didn't feel good about that, either. She wasn't big, but she certainly wasn't little. Also, someone at school had once told her she had a small head. Was that bad?

Louise did it anyway, and it looked pretty good. But she did wonder, in the weeks and months that followed, if she had made a mistake. Did the haircut magnify her asymmetrical face? Did it make her butt look bigger? Was this how she was going to spend her life, trying to minimize the obvious? Always scheming about how to look less—less like how she really was? She was getting tired of worrying about how she looked. She was getting worn down. She was starting not to care what others thought. Or maybe it wasn't about these invisible "others," maybe she was starting not to care about what she, her own worst critic, thought. Because that's who was really judging her so harshly—Louise herself. Somehow, having a baby who had left her with a stomach-pooch and stretch marks had minimized the rest of her abnormalities. Or maybe it was being a teacher—to her students she was just a married woman with a kid, whereas they were the sexy, the vibrant, the young. Even when Louise told them "I'm serious, I would never be your age again for anything," they laughed and looked at each other, but she meant it. Merely living a little bit longer had mellowed the harshness. Or had begun to, anyway.

Four or five months after she got her short haircut, Louise had a dream that she was smiling. It was a perfect, toothpaste-commercial smile, with both ends of the lips moving away from the teeth, her cheeks swelling into little apples. During the dream,

*[handwritten: Growth! Yay!]*

Louise thought, "I knew it. I knew my facial movement would come back. It was only a matter of time. Thank God." And that was it, the dream ended.

It was the kind of dream that felt so real that it took a few minutes for Louise to realize it was only a dream when she woke up. It left her feeling depressed for the better part of the day. There was nothing to do except wait for the feeling to pass—which she knew from experience, would happen. It had caught her by surprise, that dream, because she had thought she was long past wishing for the impossible, for what had happened to her face, eyes, and body to reverse itself. After all, it had been almost nine years since her brain surgeries, Louise said to herself as she rubbed some hair paste between her palms and then through her hair. She was going for that not-thought-about look her hairstylist had taught her.

This was the same hairstylist she'd had since she was 18 and had first moved to Lawrence, Kansas. Louise remembered the shock on the hairstylist's face when she first returned to the salon, having moved back to Kansas after her brain surgeries, looking very different than when she had last been there a year ago. Recently, at an appointment, her hairstylist had admitted to feeling nervous around Louise at first when she had returned.

"I wasn't sure how you would be as a person, you know? You looked different, had been through so much, I just didn't know," she said, pausing. "But then we started talking again, just like old times, and I was like, 'Oh, it's still Louise.'"

Louise thought she knew what her hairstylist was saying, that what was on her inside was still the same, even if her outside was different. She looked at her new, short hair, the dyed blond growing out and the brown coming in. Her real color, which she hadn't seen since high school. She was going to leave it, going natural.

Maybe she could be more authentic now if she stopped trying to be anything else. "Striking," Janet had called it, this new, darker color. Louise liked that.

"One evening near the end of my long separation from the mirror, I was sitting in a café talking to a man I found quite attractive when I suddenly wondered what I looked like to him. What was he actually *seeing* in me? I asked myself this old question, and startlingly, for the first time in my life, I had no ready answer. I had not looked in the mirror for so long that I had no idea what I objectively looked like. I studied the man as he spoke; for all those years I'd handed my ugliness over to people and seen only the different ways it was reflected back to me. As reluctant as I was to admit it now, the only indication in my companion's behavior was positive.

And then I experienced a moment of the freedom I'd been practicing for behind my Halloween mask all those years ago. As a child I expected my liberation to come from getting a new face to put on, but now I saw it came from shedding something, shedding my image.

I used to think truth was eternal, that once I *knew*, once I *saw*, it would be with me forever, a constant by which everything else could be measured. I know now that this isn't so, that most truths are inherently unretainable, that we have to work hard all our lives to remember the most basic things."

—**Lucy Grealy**, *Autobiography of a Face*

# How They Got Their Exercise

Depending on whom you talked to, it was either a recumbent bicycle or an adult tricycle. There was a big difference between the two terms. "Recumbent bicycle" sounded like a serious piece of machinery, and called to Louise's mind old men who wore spandex shorts and sucked packets of energy gel. "Adult tricycle," though, sounded too special, something for people who could not ride a two-wheeled bicycle, and well, who couldn't do that? It was like saying "adult crib" or "adult diaper"—something for the very old, the almost gone from this world.

*

Louise got one, though. A trike. Silver, with fenders and a big basket in the back, screaming "farmer's market." Louise took it for a ride around the block the first night she got it, wobbling the handlebars, gripping the rubber handles so hard her forearms ached. But the trike itself stayed steady.

*

The next weekend, Nick proposed going for a family ride. His bike had a child seat in the back, the same kind from when he and Louise were little. Olive tolerated it. Louise bought three helmets: black for Nick, grey for herself, and a pink one with ladybugs for Olive.

"Don't go fast," Louise said, getting on slowly, double-checking her feet position on the pedals. She didn't like following Nick when he drove a car. He always sped up at yellow lights. She had a feeling this would be similar.

"Well, I'm going to go faster than that snail's pace you've been going," Nick said.

He had seen Louise practicing the last few nights after Olive was in bed. "I'm joking," he said, seeing Louise scowl, but Louise knew she went slowly. Before she had any more time to get anxious, Nick strapped Olive in and they set off. Through the neighborhood, over the train tracks, down a road headed to the county line. Every so often Louise felt herself get off balance a little bit, and she found that she couldn't steer with just one hand, not even for a second, for instance if she had to scratch her neck or push her helmet back. But still. They were moving fast, and they were quiet. The feeling was sort of like swimming: one's clumsiness, the force of gravity pinning feet to the ground—all that didn't matter now. Louise moved forward, pedaling toward something new. In this way, she was changing.

✱

Nick took up running. At a physical, his doctor told him he had high cholesterol and needed to lose twenty pounds. He started running on the levee trail behind their house that night. He began doing one mile and soon was up to three, then five. He bought actual running shoes and clothes: New Balances, dry-wick shirts and stretchy shorts; previously he had been running in what he wore to mow the lawn. Louise was jealous. She had always been the health-conscious one of their twosome: at their favorite restaurant, he always got the fried chicken sandwich and dipped his fries in spicy mayo; she would get the black bean burger with a side salad. She liked taking spin classes but had missed the first session, when the lingo had been explained. She spent the first six weeks of the class not knowing what to do when the teacher called out "Take it to a seven!" and subsequently "Rev it up to ten!" She researched it on the Internet and finally figured it out. It had to do with resistance. Louise had a cabinet-full of exercise DVDs with titles such as *Dance the Chakras* and *Balance Ball for Weight Loss*. She took yoga and Pilates, but both were too frustrating for her, balance-wise—she kept falling over. She would try anything, but running was something she could not do. When she had to, if Olive was running too close to the street, say, she limped fast and it looked sort of like a gallop, but her right leg was not strong enough to push her forward like her left leg was. So, she was jealous of Nick's runs. At night, after they put Olive to bed and Louise was settling down on the couch with her iPad and an ice cream bar, Nick would change into his gear and kiss her on the top of the head on his way out the door. At first, she thought it was a phase and he would give it up, regaining his seat on the couch next to her with a beer in his hand. But he kept on, trading the beer for chocolate milk to be guzzled after his runs, making running playlists on his computer, and trying new stretches he read about in the running magazine he now got.

They started to fight about it. Louise would ask Nick if he wanted to watch a T.V. show and Nick would say, "Can it wait until I get back and shower?" and she would sigh. But she knew that this was not a battle worth continuing. Everyone else in their life congratulated Nick and how great he was looking, and his doctor shook his hand the next time Nick came in.

"It sucks that you can run and I can't," she said to Nick one night when they were laying on the couch as they sometimes did, whatever show they were watching finished, the screen black, knowing they should go to bed but not wanting to do the drudgeries of preparing for the morning quite yet. "Yes, it totally does," Nick said, and that was it. It was perhaps the simplest, truest thing they had ever said to each other, and it somehow allowed Louise to finally be happy for him. Sometimes the acknowledging of the situation made all the difference.

Maybe things just stayed the same. Maybe always, despite one's best efforts to evolve, to focus on what was important, you were who you were. There were times since having Olive that Louise was sure she had matured, become enlightened, even, like when she endured a half-hour tantrum stoically, cleaned a urine-soaked couch cushion for the third time in one week (Olive's potty training), or got one hour of sleep for an entire night. Life would proceed, as always, and it would all be fine. But for every moment where Louise thought she had it all figured out, there was one that showed Louise that she was exactly the same as the night she met Nick, almost nine years ago when she was 22, fresh out of the hospital.

She had been on the steps of an apartment building with her cane in one hand and a beer in the other, smoking, one lens of her glasses covered with tape so she wouldn't see double. Nick had just arrived, and he shook her hand when a friend introduced them. And that was all, that night. Nick went inside, and Louise stayed on the steps, waiting for her ex-boyfriend to come outside after his band finished playing in the apartment's living room. She was trying to get back together with this guy. They had dated a couple of years before her brain surgeries, and she dumped him for a Frenchman and a plan to move to California. But now she wanted him back. She wanted her old life back, actually, and she was going to get it, somehow.

It never happened, of course. Her ex had moved on, he told her gently later that night, and what Louise didn't even realize then was that she was beginning her new life. But she was still looking back at who she used to be, and how she could become that girl again. She was looking backwards so fixedly that she didn't even see the gift that she had just met. She had let him walk on by. Good thing she and Nick had run into each other again a week later, and again a week after that. Good thing he could see in Louise what she could not. Good thing people got more than one chance. Sometimes, though, Louise still feels exactly like that 22-year-old woman, waiting on the steps for something that will never come. She wonders when that feeling will stop.

# Notes

**Page 10:** Berger, John. *Selected Essays*. New York: Vintage International. 2003
Sontag, Susan. *On Photography*. New York: Picador. 2001.

**Page 21:** Johnson, Lacy M. *The Other Side: A Memoir*. Portland, Oregon & Brooklyn, New York: Tin House Books. 2014.

**Page 89:** Elliott, Stephen. *The Adderall Diaries: A Memoir*. Graywolf Press. 2010.

**Page 94:** Grealy, Lucy. *Autobiography of a Face*. New York: Harper Perennial. 2003.

# Acknowledgements

To my editors, Dean Rader and Jonathan Silverman, thank you for taking a chance on this book and believing in it so strongly. To my dad, Clay Stauffer (Warner), my mom, Susan Lynn (Janet), and my stepparents, Barbara Griffin and Brian Wolfe (the Doctor), in you I have as strong of a support system as ever there was, and I am so, so grateful. To Veronica Krug, and so many people from the Henry and Krug family, for being amazingly kind and supportive.

To my brothers, Tim and Aaron Stauffer (Tom and Michael), for helping me to laugh at myself. To Violeta Stauffer Rodriguez for always being ready to celebrate with me. I am so glad you moved here. To Lauren, thank you for being such an amazing aunt to Olive and Bruce, and partner to my brother.

To my teachers Joe Harrington, Laura Moriarty, Tom Lorenz, and Megan Kaminski, thank you so much for believing in this book before it was a book. Your guidance and advice kept me working and kept my faith in this project strong. I couldn't have done it without you all. Thank you to Deb Olin Unferth for being a resource and guiding figure, I know I can always call you.

To Jennifer Colatosti, a brilliant writer, a devoted reader of many, many drafts of the pieces, and a true-blue friend whom I can count on the see the lamest (best!) chick-flicks and go shopping for absolutely anything—I am grateful for you. To Jennifer Pacioianu, thank you for reading whatever I could offer, and for giving heart-felt advice and guidance on what to do with the scraps I sent you.

And last but always first, to Nick, Olive, and Bruce. You three are what keep me going, and I hope I bring you one-zillionth of the happiness you bring me.

These essays have previously appeared in slightly different forms in the following publications: "The Mind 440" in *Parcel*; "Trice" in *River Teeth*; "ESFJ" in *Paragraphiti*; "Imagine Yourself as a Mother" in *Echoes From the Prairie: A Collection of Short Memoirs*. The author wishes to thank the editors of these publications.